T H E
BLACK CLOAK

By R. S. Wilkinson

PAGE PUBLISHING, INC.
New York, NY

First originally published by Page Publishing, Inc. 2016

Cover by: Sandra Esty Burt

ISBN 978-1-68289-137-7 (pbk)
ISBN 978-1-68289-138-4 (digital)

Printed in the United States of America

CONTENTS

PREFACE

The Black Cloak

The title refers to The Black Cloak of disapproval and sometimes Guilt which I have shared with my brother, Dave, from infancy until now.

These stories are true. The names have not been changed to protect the guilty. The chronology is as accurate as my records, letters and memory will allow. The stories range over a span of eighty years—1935—2015. There are very few "stretchers"…in fact most of the events are understated.

The cast of characters includes family and friends and students and enemies and even some dubious relatives:

Dan, my younger brother—three years younger—still at 77 playing the banjo and performing with the likes of Billy Dean, Spyro Gyra, Dolly Parton, Smoking Woodstove among "others." The "others" cover much ground. We started playing together as 11 and 14 year old campers at Camp Chewonki, performing the great song featuring a cow with twenty-seven spigots: "Pass the Other Udder."

My sister, Peggy, seven years older; brothers: Dave, four years older; and Sam, nine years older than I; all now deceased, are included in the stories.

Mother, Margaret Jones Wilkinson, slightly older than I—by about forty years—known for almost fifty years as Grammy. Mother taught us manners, behavior, respect, and that she did not make mistakes and was never wrong. As children this gave us great security—someone had to be right.

Dad, Dr. Samuel Allen Wilkinson, Jr.—President of American Gastroenterological Society while on staff at the Lahey Clinic, 1957, who taught me among other things to be independent, play Chess and appreciate classical music and to tell the truth.

Friend: Bob Stein,—with whom I tried to grow up.

Teachers and administrators are named as they appear and disappear.

Most stories are in chronological order, except for the last chapter which does jump around.

ANY RESEMBLANCE TO THE LIVING OR DEAD IS ENTIRELY TRUE...UNLESS YOU WISH TO APPLY JOSEPH CONRAD'S "TRUE LIE"...WHICH I LEAVE UP TO YOU... And, you must read the book to find out what I am talking about.

I have left out many people, mostly on purpose, including: Erika, my first wife who says she: "is not bad for an old chicken."

My children: Heather, Russel and Grace: born in 1959, 1961 and 1962 are included but not featured in these stories. They will be in my next book about how we lived and farmed and survived without electricity for eighteen years in West Newfield, Maine.

And saved the best for last: Claire, my wife, whom I met while listening to Jazz and avoiding Brahma bulls, has been with me for fifty years. I am obsessed with "Reason" and the "Truth", am very stubborn, and a genius who has been interested in money but never compromising to get it, am hard to live with. But Claire is smarter than I – her IQ and earthy awareness have made her more than a match, everyman's dream. She is still my fun girl, and that is another story…

BABIES THINK

RS Wilkinson

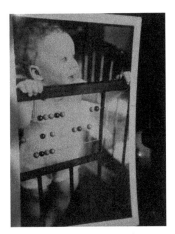

planning crib jailbreak-1935

My first jailbreak: the start of the Black Cloak.

WE ALL KNOW THAT BABIES THINK. My earliest thoughts that I can clearly remember now go back to when I was 6 months old. I recall two events, accomplishments, from that wonderful age. The first memory involves breaking the code on my crib. Those days, 1935, were the days of the proper crib: a hard mattress surrounded with jail-like wooden bars that were spaced just far enough apart to almost squeeze my head through. The objective was to keep the pesky little dudes and dudettes confined at a less than backbreaking height...out of harm's way and in a bedroom with a closed door so that mommy and daddy could get some sleep and have sex in private. Mother said I was a "difficult" baby.

It started when I observed that the way to get out of crib-jail involved lowering the sliding side rail. Mother would pick up one foot, put her toe on the trip lever under the bed and push down on the lever which released the side rail and allowed it to lower several inches, making it easier for her to reach me. The rail, unless carefully held, would drop with a loud bang, sliding on two steel tubes which ran through holes drilled in the upper and lower part of the railing—a brilliantly simple mechanism. But to my six month old mind it was a challenge worthy of hours of study and observation. Watching Mother as she made her many, many feeding, cleaning and checking-up-on-me checks, I finally got it: push that lever under the side of the mattress and it would lower the railing. I had no way of knowing what was to follow. Reaching the lever was the next challenge.

It took many tries. For at least a week it was my only activity other than the normal crying for food or attention, and I had conquered that stuff. Finally, by lying on my stomach, sticking my arm, shoulder and head between two bars and curling the toes of my right foot around the nearest railing bar and pushing with all of my might, I moved the retaining lever enough to disengage it. CRASH! The railing dropped almost ten inches and stopped just a fraction short of my head. This scared me, and I rolled away from the side of the crib and was lying innocently motionless in the center of my mattress when Mother ran in and instantly picked me up and clutched me to her breast. Not what I had expected, but not a bad result. I later heard that this prompted an investigation of the crib—it was found to be working perfectly, and the conclusion was that Bobby was trying a jailbreak. This was my beginning...the first recorded wearing of the "Black Cloak"...infant size!

Well actually the Black Cloak "thing" started at about five months! I had the habit of vigorously drinking my bottle and then throwing it out of the crib. Undoubtedly this was a result of the weaning crisis. Although we were breast fed until about 18 month of age, Mother started weaning us at five months. My reaction to the rubber nipple and glass bottle replacement of the real thing was to gulp down the milk and throw (Mother used the term "fling") the bottle out of the crib. This necessitated lining the floor with blankets to prevent the bottles from breaking. It also saved some of my brains from concussions when I started jail-breaking—which was my next act.

Lowering the railing was indeed only the beginning. I sensed that I was making too much commotion when I dropped the side rail, and discovered that by pushing my pillow through the bars at one end of the bed, it would cushion the dropping side rail, and, "AHA"—no noise. Also of extreme importance and annoyance to others, at six months I was already walking. True, it was a staggering, jerky, out-of-control-lurching-walk, ending with a crash to the floor. Occasionally for variety I added in pulling down a table lamp or smashing something left on a coffee table as I reeled around clutching for control. And although I assure you that none of this was malicious, it was indeed fun. Following development of the rail-dropping skill, my next act of incredible un-coordination was to pull myself over the lowered crib railing, swing my diapered rear over the edge, and fall noisily to the floor and freedom. Mother actually gave up trying to contain me and lined the area around the crib with pillows—which lessened the blood and brain damage involved in my jailbreaks.

According to Mother and Dad, at one year old I would quietly lower the crib railing, thump down onto the floor, and toddle into their bedroom every morning at 4 AM, staggering to the end of the bed, clutching and yanking spasmodically on their blanket for support, looking up with those big, wide-open baby eyes and say: "Go back a-bed Bobby," and then turn and go back to my bedroom to mess with my toys which had been thrown out of the crib… undoubtedly for easy access to me. And yes, I could talk too and was simply repeating the every-morning, sleepy greeting that Mother had so often given me.

As kids our almost non-stop energy led us to delight in mischief: we were always edging over the line of accepted behavior, and, possibly because we were not allowed to interrupt adults, we did not presume to offer our un-asked for opinions, and we were not allowed to whine or complain…we gave the appearance of being good listeners, and were never bored. I do not recall ever hearing anyone say, "I'm bored." Oh yes, we were sometimes lonely, scared, frightened, unsure, and tired along with all of the good emotions, but we were not bored.

Finally, the "Black Cloak" was shared over the years as a mark of distinction…as my brother Dave, who competed with me for ownership, said; "We were either being good or bad—which was all fun. As long as you use your brain, how could you be bored? We could always think of something 'unacceptable' to do."

GIRLS

RS Wilkinson

Girls were challenging for me…especially at seven years old. They didn't play like boys, they didn't run like boys, they didn't yell like boys, they didn't understand anything about secret club passwords or covering your back with lies, and could not be trusted to keep any secret at all…not even for two days! They often squealed the whole program to adults…yup tattletales—the worst of all traits. Anything looking like approval of a girl was totally forbidden—we never admitted that we liked a girl…never. Except, maybe to one trusted, best friend, and even he could not really be trusted with this information.

The first girl I secretly liked was Sally. She lived next door, well actually two doors away. And she was smart—as near as I could tell, all girls were smart. They got A's from teachers I didn't even like… actually I only liked about one teacher each year, all through grade school, which was a long, long time…as far ahead as I could even imagine. I'll get back to teachers, but Sally was neat. She ran all gangly-legged—feet splaying out to the sides, kind of rocking left and right, and her smile went across and then down at the corners without showing her teeth, which made her brown eyes look alive with mischief, and as if they were miles deep, way deep. When she was closer than three feet away, my legs felt strangely rubbery, and the pit of my stomach hurt.

And Sally was helping me chase lightening bugs on Saturday, June 6, 1942–a day I clearly remember. The bugs were low-flying in the lilacs on the edge of our back yard, and I tried to show off by jumping up to catch one in my hand, and amazingly I caught one! Sally said, "Give it to me, and I will do you a favor." I opened my hand a little and the lightening bug lit up and glowed for a second or two. Sally placed her hand over mine and gently closed her fingers to capture the bug. We stared silently, and then without thinking, I blurted out: "I'll show you mine if you'll show me yours." Sally looked at me, eyes wide open while her face changed from innocent joy to wrinkles between her eyebrows to tight-lipped concentration to a slight, curled up, at the corners of her lips, tight smile. And she nodded ever so slightly. Then she slowly opened her hand, pursed her lips and gently blew the tiny glowing bug into freedom.

I had never thought of doing this before—girls were off limits—we had no clue what they looked like, really. "Sex" was not discussed; it was never even mentioned by our parents or any other adult, and all we knew was that it was forbidden to even talk about it, therefor we didn't know anything except that girls were different, and it was whispered that they were missing a penis...I had bragged that I actually knew what our "thing" was called because Mother had told me to stop calling it a "hoser," and she said it was a penis so this must be true. I really didn't like Mother's name for it..."hoser" sounded much better to my ear. But knowing the correct name for it was big news around the neighborhood, and at this moment with Sally, I was thinking that if I could actually say that I had seen what a girl looked like I would be the "man" and what is more important, the only "man" in my age group.

So I undid my belt, unbuttoned my fly (we had buttons in those days) and pushed my pants and drawers halfway down to my knees which were trembling. Sally was staring, bent over, hands on her knees, feet spread, and then she covered her mouth with her right hand, pointed with her left hand, and started to giggle. Suddenly she turned and ran off toward her house, and she was gone.

Sadly, Sally never spoke to me again, and of course, I never did see hers'. We never chased lightening bugs again. I never even saw her at school because she was so smart that she skipped two grades and was not in the same class. But I will eternally remember her, and she taught me three things that left lasting conclusions: girls are unpredictable, enchanting, and some of them can be trusted, even with a secret—I know this because Sally never told anyone about my exposure: if she had, in my neighborhood, I would have heard about it.

"YOU BEAST!"

RS Wilkinson

Mother called out as I hit Dan over the head with a feather-light, rotten, larch tree branch. The branch disintegrated into a cloud of wood dust, and Dan, unfazed but hearing Mother's call from her watch post in the kitchen window, seized the opportunity and faked a beautiful eye-roll-fallback-onto-the-ground-into-a Christ-on-the-cross position.

Dan held his position, pretending a complete knockout, extracting the most possible sympathy from Mother. Although he did not even have an egg (do you remember eggs?? The egg-like bump that we treated with ice on the head...yes, probably for concussions of which we had many.)

I looked in dismay at my wrecked town. The cause of the altercation was that Dan had "stumbled" into a "town" that I had spent all afternoon building, which included a miniature brick road, a tent made with a handkerchief and twigs, several toy people, a twig house, and our homemade fire engine, and he had kicked it all into smithereens. This, of course could not be tolerated, and my ten year old mind required instant justice and revenge...thus the larch branch punishment was enacted.

Courts of law are not about justice. Any lawyer will tell you this, and neither was the credible witness's misinterpretation of the facts as I saw them. And even worse, Mother was the credible witness. My goose was cooked and I knew so was my rear end, my 25 cent allowance, and my listen to the Lone Ranger permit, which had allowed me to stay up until 9:00 PM on Fridays. The world had crashed.

On Dan there was no evidence, no blood, no egg-like bump, no tears, the sting was near-perfect. Brother Dave, who was 4 years older than I, and who resented having to sometimes take his younger brother, meaning me, with him, was truly happy to see my suffering and said:" Now you get to wear the Black Cloak and see how that feels!!"

To compound and further cement my family position, Mother further testified that I had called my innocent younger brother a "Bastard! This is true. I had done this, because although I did not know the meaning of the word, I had heard it used effectively at the playground. The word had a phonetic punch to it—had strength and the ability to elicit strong reactions—so I used it emphatically on Dan.

That really did it…I was a foul-mouthed bully.

The lowest of the low…instructed never to hit, strike, yell at, or in any way to abuse my younger brother, which, to me, was impossible. And I recall thinking "The little Bastard really got away with it this time!"

So much for repentance.

And alone, banished to my room, waiting for Dad to return from work with further punishment, I turned to my only consistent, faithful and loyal friend and masturbated.

THE 360...

RS Wilkinson

Long before seatbelts, airbags, anti-lock brakes—in the days of bench seats and add-on, bolted-to-the- steering-column directional signals—and even before Mother had a driver's license, almost the whole family: Peg, Dave, Dan and I were riding in the back seat of our nearly new 1947 Desoto. We had just reached the foothills in the White Mountains of NH. Dad had driven us up to the peak of Mt. Washington, which of course was in the clouds.

Dad was a good driver. I remember riding with him in our 1940 Ford—the starter button on the floor to the right of the gas pedal and the headlight low-beam switch on the floor to the left of the clutch fascinated me—they were not to be touched. I also remember, at four years old, how I fell out of the car when Dad was turning left: the door swung open and I rolled off the seat and landed on the running board...sitting with my feet dangling just above the road until Dad reached over, grabbed my arm and hoisted me back into the seat. He slowed, pulled the door shut, and said: "Don't tell your mother about this," patted my knee, and all was well with me and the world. It was a secret I willingly kept for 75 years. It was a close call, but it was nothing compared to the amazing, near-death experiences that surround my Mother's driving.

Yes, in 1947 Dad completed the trip up Mt. Washington safely, and we were in the foothills when Mother spoke the most-feared words: "I would like to drive for a while." Mother was short, 5'2", and needed a cushion too see over the steering wheel…it was before adjustable seat heights too!

"I don't think we brought the cushion with us," said Dad.

"I put it in the trunk," replied Mother. And that was that.

Dad pulled off the road, retrieved the cushion, and Mother sat at attention, staring straight ahead, clutching the wheel with an I-mean-business death-grip. Squished together in the back seat, we four silent, prisoners clenched our cheeks and prepared for the worst. The Desoto had fluid drive, a two speed transmission which shifted from a very weak lower gear to an even weaker higher gear. To start off there was a soft clutch that had a spongy engagement, coupled with a flat-head six cylinder capable of reaching sixty in about 40 seconds of agonizing urging. . Although it was almost impossible to do this, Mother managed to lurch forward by racing the motor and releasing the clutch and then instantly hitting the brake with her left foot while keeping the accelerator floored. This caused the car to sit on its haunches then nose dive—a perfectly normal start for Mother, as we bounced off of the back seat and then lurched forward into the back of the front seat.

Upon reaching driving speed, about 45 mph, Mother settled into her super control mode: constant left- right-left-right steering, expertly combined with acceleration for two seconds, and then deceleration for two seconds. The smile on her face told us that everything was going as planned, and we grimaced, fought down car-sickness and prepared for the worst. It was mercifully quick.

After lurching successfully around several curves, Mother ramped up the speed to 55 mph as we approached a sharp curve. She confidently believed that a car should turn if you turned the steering wheel, and it should stop if you hit the brake, it was simple…Speed had nothing to do with controlling an automobile…a good car was supposed to go where you aimed it. So, with squealing tires we slid off of the road onto a large gravel approach and parking area leading to a small (two pump) gas station.

The pumps stood about 30 feet from the small station house, and we were sliding directly toward the pumps. I remember watching the gas station attendant running away from the pumps, head down, arms pumping furiously, heading for the small house. As the car slid in a horrible, awkward, noisy spin, with gravel and dust churning in spectacular audio-visual style...all of us hit the floor—four kids piled on top of each other...Dan and Dave were on the bottom, and Peg and I fought for positions of safety on top of the pile, and finally, not daring to watch the bitter end, we closed our eyes and ducked; we were trapped in the slow, almost frozen, nightmare speed of "I'm gonna die any second." But the car rocked to a stop, having completed a 360 degree spin, and we were alive, and we hadn't hit anything, and I looked up, and the gas station attendant was standing...frozen in place...up against the side of the station house, eyes wide open with a deer-in-the-headlights look.

Dad eased out of the car, walked through the dust cloud, around to the driver's side, looked down at Mother and quietly said, "Move over."

As Mother handed Dad the pillow and slid over to the passenger's side, she looked innocently up and said: "Well you know, I turned the wheel and,—and they just shouldn't make cars that won't go where you aim them!!"

STALEMATE, AND THE PAINFUL TRUTH

RS Wilkinson

I don't know why Dad chose to play chess with me. I was eleven when he taught me how to set up the board with the rhyming key: square on the right must always be white, and queen and her square, same colored pair. He showed me how the players moved. How each player had its unique options and limitations, and he told me that most great leaders and thinkers had enjoyed playing chess, and that it would teach me how to think ahead. I did not know what thinking ahead meant, but Dad said that it was a rare skill…that most present day leaders didn't seem to do it much. The year was 1946, and because World War II had ended a year ago, we were almost back to "normal".

I knew Dad had served in World War 1 in the US Army, was a sergeant, had been wounded, hit with shrapnel from an exploding mortar as he was restoring radio antennas which were on the top of a stone building which the Germans were shelling. He was knocked unconscious, (his old helmet had a dent in it) he inhaled mustard gas which had been lobbed up onto the rooftop, recovered enough to roll down the stairs leading to the rooftop, and his buddies treated him, saved him. He was barely eighteen years old. He was never the same. Nobody who has seen action is ever the same. Dad was telling me about his war experience as he explained the game of chess. He said the chess piece that is called a "castle" looked much like the structure he was on top of when he was hit. He knew the risk he was taking, but he did not have anyone watching him, covering him. He was lucky not to be killed. Then he explained that in chess you must always "cover" your players who are exposed as a result of your moving them into either attacking or retreating positions.

Dad was a really good chess player. He taught me the basic moves and two openings and that was it. I was on my own. We played at least two games per week over a period of five years, and I wish I had listened more closely to what he said, but often we just concentrated...for two or three hours...quiet concentration, what a great, useful skill to be taught. As for the winning—well I never beat Dad. I did manage several "stalemates" (a tie), but I never won, a "mate." I guess he always felt that I should truly earn whatever I might achieve: premonitions of the Bicycle and First Car stories.

Later, in 1954, he told me the story of Ted Williams. That's right, the great baseball player...many think the greatest hitter ever. Dad was a Doctor, practicing at the Lahey Clinic in Boston, and he had Ted Williams as a patient. We were Red Sox fans, and Dad had several interesting talks with at least three of the great baseball players: Ted Williams, Yogi Berra and Ty Cobb. All were patients of Dad, (I once had autographed baseballs from them, but only the Ty Cobb ball remains in my possession). I remember saying that I thought they were all "naturally great athletes" and Dad disagreed. He said Ted told him that he kept a baseball bat with him everywhere he went, and that before he went to bed, every night, he took at least one hundred swings. Ted said: "To excel at anything for more than an instant takes long-term concentration...you have to dedicate your mind to it and your body will follow." Dad agreed.

Ted served in the Korean War. That was the war of the 38th parallel...the U.S. troops were not allowed to cross over that parallel into enemy territory, but the enemy repeatedly crossed over this line and blasted us. We could chase the enemy to the 38th th parallel but could not cross that line even in pursuit. Ted flew a jet...and was shot down. He lived through this experience and returned to Boston after the war, once again to play baseball for the Boston Red Sox. His comment to Dad and the press was: "It was the stupidest war—a waste of lives to fight a war that could not be won…a stalemate at best. Imagine being in a fight where your opponent draws a line of chalk on the floor and says: "I can cross over the line and hit you and throw stuff at you, but you can only retaliate up to the line—you can't even chase me over the line. You can't possibly win."

It was explained to all of us that "holding the line" was considered a victory…Ted did make a statement to the press and was told by the powers that be that if he ever expected to play baseball again he must apologize—retract his statement. Ted did this: he really had no choice. This taught me a true lesson: Never criticize A if you want to get a job with B. Perhaps a variation of the true lie?

Dad was a truly great doctor. I know this because I lived with him for 24 years. Even though he had an office in the Lahey Clinic, he made house calls, as did many of the doctors practicing at the Clinic. A gastroenterologist, far ahead of his time as a healer, he believed he had failed if a patient of his needed surgery. He was constantly recommending changes in diet. He thoroughly understood how different foods were digested and assimilated. In 1951 he warned me that antibiotics should not be used except in serious or life threatening cases. In 1953 he invited to dinner a friend, Doctor Paul Dudley White, the foremost cardiologist in the country…The conversation is still fresh in my memory:

> Dr. White was speaking about his long past experience: "I was just starting my medical career, serving as a doctor during World War I, and I performed many autopsies on our soldiers. Many of them were in their early twenties when they were killed. The most interesting thing to me was how clean their cardio vascular systems were: no plaque—not even a sign of it. These were kids raised on bacon and eggs, whole, unpasteurized and un-homogenized milk, you know, the kind that had the cream on top…and lots of beef and

pork, and lard in the crusts of their butterfat and sugar-loaded pies...but no plaque in their arteries."

I was eighteen years old. No one interrupted an adult in those days. Even other adults did not interrupt each other, we listened. Complete sentences were the norm.

Dr. White continued: "I also performed autopsies on soldiers who were killed in World War Two, and the twenty year-olds had significant plaque in their arteries. I took note of this as a cardiologist, but had no idea what had caused such a noticeable change between 1920 and 1945. Then during the Korean War, 1950—1953, I also autopsied soldiers aged eighteen to twenty-two and was amazed at the startling increase in plaque—even in the eighteen year olds. So I set out to find an answer to this."

We were all quiet, he had our complete attention. Even Dad, the gastroenterologist, did not venture guesses or interrupt.

Dr. White continued: "I asked what changes in diet had almost universally occurred in the U.S. between World War One and World War Two and finally hit upon an answer...the homogenization of milk. I investigated and found that the change that occurs in milk during the homogenization process which prevents the cream or fat from rising to the top, cannot be broken down by our bodies." Dr. White looked at us, I think to see if we were getting it, so I nodded, and he continued: "Put simply, the butter fat that no longer separates in milk because it is homogenized, involves a process that cannot be reversed by the human body, and it is not truly digested, and it stays within us in our arteries contributing to the formation of arterial plaque. I further discovered that the same is true of hydrogenated oils that are found in so many foods. Hydrogenated oils became extremely popular when, during WWII, butter was rationed and oleomargarine was introduced as a substitute. Now many foods contain hydrogenated or partially hydrogenated oils. The body simply can't separate and eliminate or discharge the extra hydrogen atom in hydrogenated foods. This also adds to the arterial problem as a component of plaque."

I clearly recall being astounded. ""We need to tell everybody about this!" I exclaimed. I expected to be admonished for my outbreak. Instead, Dr. White smiled warmly at my boyishly honest outburst and said: "It is not that simple. Think of the huge industries that would be affected by this. The money involved is astronomical, and I am sure I would be discredited—perhaps considered a quack. No, I am afraid I shall never speak of this in public."

And that concluded that conversation and dinner. The subject was never broached again.

As Dr. White left he, smiled knowingly at Dad, who silently nodded.

I was learning the awesome power, the frustrating uselessness and the fear of the "truth." Since that day I have, upon countless occasions, kept my mouth shut. The truth, I have found, is so powerful that those who profit by deception will actually destroy, even kill, to prevent it. I had "learned" this in 1952 when Bill Kenney, my French teacher had told me after the "Spectator" incident: "Stick you little neck out…chop, chop." (Explained in "The Spectator" chapter.)

Dad did have a heart attack in 1953 and Dr. White became his doctor. I am sure Dad's 'attack' was caused mostly by lingering ill effects of his WWI service. Both he and Dr. White were strong advocates of good diets, exercise and preventive medicine. Among other notable achievements, Dr. White was appointed as President Eisenhower's personal physician in 1955. Although there is still debate about his theory regarding homogenization, his stance regarding the ill effects of hydrogenation is generally accepted.

This all actually applies to the game of Chess—you need to anticipate reactions and cover your moves, and often what looks like a good move is disastrous in the long run, and if the players are skillful, you will be lucky to achieve a "Stalemate." However if you win, ah yes, there's the rub!

Ironically, in Chess as in war, to win you must destroy all or almost all that is of value in your enemy as you strive to checkmate the King, the symbol of power, control, ownership and success. Also ironically the King can only move one space at a time. The other

players do all of the work, the battle. They take the risks while pro-
tecting the King. The king is almost useless in battle. Joseph Conrad
understood this when he wrote <u>Heart of Darkness</u>: a book in which
he also included examples of his fascinating theories involving the
"true lie" and the "flabby devil" which were theories whose validity
has been proven correct...as I have repeatedly observed during my
lifetime. And what are these theories? Well as clearly as I can put it:
the True Lie is a lie that is told and/or perpetrated because telling the
truth will do more harm than good.

An example of the True Lie occurs at the very end of <u>Heart of
Darkness </u>as Marlow tells Kurtz's fiancée: his "Intended" that Marlow's
last word was that he spoke her name. It would have destroyed her to
know his actual last word(s): "The horror, the horror," and there was
no good of any kind that would result from telling the truth. Hence
the ironic goodness of the "true lie" which had to remain buried in
Marlow's heart of darkness...wherein lies part of the meaning of the
heart of darkness.

And yes, the Flabby Devil is also involved in this book. How
easily we grow into accepting, then become accustomed to, and
finally promote doing nothing when we do know there is much that
needs to be done...the Flabby Devil. It is far easier to withhold the
truth, and procrastination does not immediately endanger and can
be supported by excuses, fears or just plain laziness. Thus the Flabby
Devil wins again. For more explicit information and example read
the beginning of <u>Heart of Darkness</u> up through the pages describing
the sunken steamboat and the rivets. In a world of instant gratification, computers, I-phones and I-watches (all of which will seem slow
and archaic in fifty years). I have enjoyed the slow pace and thought-
fulness provoked and required in reading. Perhaps the slowness is
also some of the attraction for me attached to the game of Chess. The
trouble is committing the time for a chess game.

...Except when I play with Bradley. Bradley is my great, great
nephew...12 years old. His parents, Allen and Carolyn and his sister,
Ashley, were visiting us last summer, and I suggested we play a game
of Chess. Bradley looked at me and said:" You won't be disappointed
by playing me." I should have known he would tell the truth because

earlier that day he had told me that he had mistakenly changed the setting on the furnace thermostat thinking it was a light switch. He said he was sorry that he had done this, and he hoped that it wouldn't cause a problem. This he confessed to me without my asking or even noticing that there might be a problem. He felt the need to tell the truth. I was and am impressed. And so we set up the game and played. Bradley quickly beat me…easily! Yes, I was out of practice, but it was no contest. I have since learned that he often plays Chess, and is so skilled that he removes some of his 'players' before starting to play just to keep the game interesting. Perhaps, if I live to be ninety and practice, I will be able to give him a run-for- the- money. Also, if I live to be ninety, I will have the pleasure of knowing him as an adult.

Bradley is unique in another way: he talks in complete sentences. Yes, that is unusual today. Try listening to TV: the news comes in incomplete sentences delivered by three or four or five people all contributing, often interrupting, taking turns, as is the format and rhythm of most TV programs and shows. Listen—every third, fourth or fifth word is emphasized in a string of interruptions and incomplete sentences. And perhaps it is the silence, even the slowness that makes reading a book refreshing for me. I can even write on the pages and flip forward and/or back, earmark special pages or sections, and the book won't crash or be easily deleted. What a great invention.

And with Dad and Dr. White, there in plain sight was the True Lie, and even the Flabby Devil, and the game of Chess, and I had learned that even very "good" people were bent into quiet patience. One of my favorite stories: "The Elephant's Child" has revisited me often since as a little boy it was read to me by my sister, Peggy. Written by Rudyard Kipling in 1900, I love this story because in contrast to Conrad's world of adult darkness and deception, Kipling wrote about the joy of discovery. The discoveries are humorous, often seemingly accidental, but the discoveries are very useful—especially in "The Elephant's Child." What seriously endangered the baby elephant was its " 'satiable curtiosity". Even now I find that insatiable curiosity will get me into trouble…and it always has. Many people whom I have known feel it is much better, certainly safer, to not ask the tough questions: "What does the Crocodile have for dinner?" is a question in the story that evokes a loud "Hush!" and a spanking…"immediately and directly without stopping for a long time." And that, dearly beloved, is just the beginning, as you will find out if you read the story. Yes, the truth can very painful, but the baby elephant becomes empowered by it and uses it as a source of strength and as a weapon. And so, at eighty I still love this story, and occasionally play chess, ask lots of questions and make people uncomfortable, and I also tell jokes—lots of jokes because it is good to smile, to laugh. And there is enough pain in life, and sometimes asking questions is truly painful, but like the elephant's nose which never returned to "normal" and became extremely useful, even powerful, so it is with the truth.

KLUSH

RS Wilkinson

"Klush" was Dave's story. It was 1945. The war had just ended. Dinner was almost over, and Dave started his war story about Joe Klushmaker. Dave's personality was magnetic—especially at fifteen. His voice was magic, mischief and music…so we listened. All eight of us, not interrupting…literally spellbound…

"Joe Klushmaker was drafted into the military, and when he reported to the induction sergeant, he put down his occupation as 'Klushmaker'. The sergeant asked him what branch of service he would like to choose. We all know this never happens, but the sergeant had never inducted a klushmaker. So Joe said he would like to be in the Navy…in a submarine. "No problem," said the sergeant, "And we'll skip basic training too—I am sure the submarine captain will be thrilled to have a klushmaker on board." And so he was. Joe was given the first mate's quarters, and was asked what he might like to do? Joe said that he wanted to read comic books—all day—that was all.

"This he was allowed to do…after a week, the captain asked Joe if he was happy, and Joe said yes, but he had run out of comic books, and he asked to be transferred to a Battleship so that he could have a bigger supply of comic books. The captain immediately complied, and Joe was transferred to a battleship with a storeroom full of comic books.

For ten weeks Joe was happy, but then he ran out of comic books, and he mentioned to the Captain that perhaps he could be transferred to an aircraft carrier in order to have his comic books flown in hot off the press…"Certainly, Joe, I am sure the Vice-Admiral on the aircraft carrier will be honored to have you", was the immediate response. And so it was that Joe had his comic books flown in weekly…and he was happy. And all he did all day was read comic books, and no one complained about him…everybody loved Joe.

"Well, it came to pass"—Dave loved to use Biblical phrases and misused big words—"That the Vice Admiral mentioned to Joe that the Admiral was visiting the ship in two weeks for an especially cadaverous inspection…and would it be possible for Joe to make a "Klush" for the occlusion? " Joe said, yes, of course, but, I will need twenty men to help me, and the use of one of the airplane elevators, and complete security—no one can watch what I am doing except the twenty helpers, and they must be isosilated from the rest of the crew.

The Vice Admiral agreed, and even though it was wartime, Joe started making a horrendous racket on the airplane elevator which was lowered to the bottom of the ship. All day came the deafening sounds of riveting, cutting of steel, hammering, welding…with huge puffs of smoke billowing up out of the bowels of the ship…all violations of the rules of secrecy surrounding the wartime locations of warships. And Joe demanded and received various parts of airplanes: wheels, propellers, parts of wings, windshields—all supplied with a smile. "Wait until the Admiral sees this," the Vice Admiral said, "No one has seen a Klush…this will surely get me a promotion to Admiral."

And the big day arrived. The sailors were all dressed in their dress Whites, standing at attention, the band was playing, and the Vice Admiral called to Joe, and Joe said he was ready. And slowly, ever so slowly, a huge crane that was used to haul up airplanes that fell into the water, hauled up a glowing mass of airplane parts. It was at least twenty feet in diameter, and Joe directed the crane operator:

"A little higher, now swing it to the left, more left, that's it, yes, over the water…now drop it! And it went KLUUUUSH!

The reactions were sensational: Mother: "Terrible, terrible, terrible."—Dad: "You wasted our time for that??"—Sam, "Disrespectable!"—Peg: "I told you they wouldn't like it"—Dan: "And then what happened?" And Bob, I was laughing so hard I peed my pants.

But this is not my story…the real story about "Klush" is about a frog! Right…a huge bullfrog that we had named Klush in honor of the story which we all loved…It started with Dan, Bobby Stein and me—six to ten years old…down at the swamp (now an upscale settlement in Brookline, Ma.) which was at the end of Clinton Rd… across Fisher Hill Ave. and down to what we called the froggyswamp. Frog hunting was an art. The frogs would be resting on lily-pads or in the grass surrounding the swamp, and they would invariably hear us coming and swim just out of range—no matter how quiet we were, they got away. It really didn't matter—it was the fun we had just messing around together…except for Klush…he had evaded us for about a month, and the challenge had to be met. We tried hitting him on the head with a stick, but we always missed. Dan ran into the swamp after it and almost caught the frog, but Dan bogged down and we hauled him out. We needed a weapon, and I proudly came up with it—a four foot long two-by-four. "Great!" we all agreed. We headed for the swamp on our bikes, and I was armed with the two-by-four. All good, except that while pedaling downhill, the weapon slipped down under my armpit and dug into the ground, which lifted me gracefully up out of my bike, hitting me in the chest, knocking the wind out of me, and crashing down together in a tangled mess, jamming between the spokes of my front wheel and bending the wheel into a "parabilic" curve—an observation solemnly offered by Bobby Stein. It took great control to restrain from bashing my co-conspirators with the two-by-four because they were all laughing at me—but I observed that I was out-numbered, and I needed their help to get home.

We did make it to the swamp on the next Saturday, and sure enough, there was Klush—sleeping in the swampgrass, about three feet from shore. We sneaked up, and BLOSH! I beaned Klush. The big frog floated still as death, and we all agreed that I had over-done it—the frog was a goner. But he was huge, and I had heard that frog's legs were supposed to be a delicacy, so we took him home. What we had not counted on was that he was "mostly dead"——not completely dead. And so, he started breathing, and by the time we got him home he was hopping mad! The unanimous decision was to put him in with "Old Moldyback" who was our pet turtle that had survived captivity all winter. Three weeks later, we released both Klush and Old Moldyback—who indeed did have a moldy look to his back—into the Elysian, froggy-turtle bog known as Stump Pond in Wakefield, New Hampshire. It is true that Dan and I still slow down on Rt. 153 in Wakefield, New Hampshire, whenever we pass Stump Pond—and nod in remembrance of Klush and Old Moldyback.

MERGATROID

RS Wilkinson

1946 was a very creative year in the automotive industry. The war was over, gasoline was no longer rationed, and Dan and I decided to go into the cart racing business. Dan was eight and I was eleven, so we really knew what we were doing. Our next door neighbor did not. Dr. Thurman looked over the chain-link fence separating our back yards and asked: "Just what are you boys making?"

"A racer," said Dan.

"Really?? I don't see any wheels," said Dr. Thurman.

Dad had recently built a table out of two-by-fours and plywood, and Dan and I had "borrowed" some of the left-over pieces of wood to make our racer. We had two three foot long pieces of two-by-four as axles and three four foot long boards, one inch thick and eight inches wide, as the chassis or platform on which we planned to sit. The rear axle was easy—just a two-by-four nailed to the boards. The front axle was made by drilling a hole through the center of the two-by-four, drilling a hole through the middle of the front edge of the cart and running a bolt through both pieces. We put three big washers between the body of the cart and the two-by-four. This allowed the axle to spin around, albeit with some resistance if the cart body was leaning left or right on the axle. And the plan was to tie ropes to the end of the axle and steer left and right by pulling on the ropes. It had taken three days to borrow the pieces needed, to cut the wood using Dad's handsaw and to start the assembly.

Dr. Thurman was right, we had no wheels. "We're going to take some off of this old fire engine that Sam had," I slowly said. We were suspicious of any help offered by an adult. Sam, our oldest brother, was almost twenty years old—incomprehensibly old—and he would not like our using the wheels off his antique toy. Actually we had no intention of using his wheels—I just said this not to appear stupid to an adult.

"I have an old baby carriage that has some pretty good wheels on it…if you can figure out how to use them; I'll give them to you." Immediately we liked Dr. Thurman a lot. He had hardly spoken to us since Dan had thrown rocks through his garage windows. That event had occurred last year, when I told Dan: "I bet you can't throw a rock over the garage…" Dan wound up with all his might and the rock went through one of the small panes in the top of the garage door. He was fascinated by the sound of breaking glass, so he threw about ten more rocks through the windows. I, of course, watched this with glee, knowing that Dan would be in big trouble when this was discovered. Unfortunately my brain had failed again to understand my obligation and responsibility to keep Dan out of trouble. Hence, the wrath of Dr. Thurman, and much worse, Dad and Mother descended upon me. Dad paid to fix the windows, and I was assigned extra chores and a reduced birthday present—a small box of fishing lures, which I recall vividly, were useless.

Therefore Dr. Thurman's offer was a pleasant surprise, and we heartily accepted. The wheels were beautiful—about twelve inches in diameter with solid rubber tires. They came with nuts and bolts and had real wheel bearings. The bolts, axle/bolts, went through the wheels and stuck out about six inches and had nuts threaded onto the ends. We measured the protruding bolt length, drilled a hole into the end of the two-by-four six inches deep and then drilled another bigger hole into the side of the two-by-four, six inches from the end, which met the end of the axle hole. Then we placed a nut and washer into the big hole, inserted the axle into its hole until it met the nut, turned the axle to tighten the nut securely and amazingly it worked!

The wheel spun smoothly. We tightened the nut onto the end of the axle, and the cart…er, racer, rolled like a champ.

"You know they won't let that thing into the Soapbox Derby looking like that," observed Sam. "You need a body, a seat, and bumpers—and where is the brake?"

"That's tomorrow's job," Dan and I said in unison.

Actually we didn't have a clue, but I remembered that in the a western movie, The Virginian, starring Gary Cooper, it showed wagon wheels being braked with a wooden block rubbing against the wheel. "I have it," I called to Dan. "We'll nail a stick to the body of Mergatroid, a few inches from the wheel so that when you push on it, it will rub against the wheel and be a brake". (We had named the racer Mergatroid after a long argument, settled by flipping a coin.) The name candidates were: Matilda, named after our washing machine; Clarabelle; Mabel (after a girl I liked); and of course, Mergatroid, a name we thought we invented.

Pushing the stick against the wheel worked fine in our back yard test—we were ready. The test run was not announced to any adults and we had no on-lookers—the slight chance of a failure followed by the certainty of finger-pointing and public embarrassment meant we maintain absolute secrecy for the first run. So together we –pulled and pushed Mergatroid up Druce St. from Clinton Rd. to the top of Fisher Hill—a distance of at least a mile…a steep grade, crossing two busy Streets, Dean Rd. and Buckminster Ave. Finally, huffing, groaning and sweating, with Dan's sneaker falling off when a wheel rolled over his foot as we lost control and the contraption almost got away and rolled back down the hill, and with Dan complaining that his "pumps" were failing and he was about to die, we reached the top at Hyslop Rd.

I instructed Dan, "You get onto the back, keep your feet on the pavement and keep the brake on, and I will get on the front, test the steering, and when I tell you to, pick up your feet and move the stick so that the brake is off." What could possibly have been more clear than these instructions? However, Dan immediately picked up his feet and released the pressure on the brake; we started rolling instantly, gathering speed, and I had no steering control.

"YOU IDIOT!" I yelled, an expression often employed during those wonderful days of accurate description preceding the euphemistic, politically correct, Pablum served up now.

Realizing he had messed-up big time, Dan dropped his feet to the ground which instantly forced him up and forward into a sort- of hump-leap and crashed him into my head and back. His feet oddly turned up onto their toes then shot out to the sides, then he held them straight out to the side, inches above the ground. I pulled on the steering ropes and at least we were going straight and I did have some control.

Our first cross street, Buckminster, was coming up; our speed was at least fifteen MPH and increasing as we neared the steepest part of the hill. I yelled: "Dan, put on the brake!" For a few seconds I heard a scraping noise, then nothing. We were really moving now. "Dan!" I yelled again, and looked to my right. Dan was holding the brake lever up in his hand because it had pulled loose from the racer body. The old expression: "up shit's creek without a paddle" took on new meaning. I knew we were doing over 20MPH and approaching the Dean Rd. crossing. The wind was blowing like a gale in my face, and the cart started to make a whistling noise. I concentrated on keeping the steering ropes tight, but they kept tugging me left and right as we went over imperfections in the road. There were no stop signs and surely no one would be looking for deranged boys riding a baby-carriage-cart.

The road flattened out somewhat for about fifty feet as we streaked across the intersection, a car sliding sideways flashed into my peripheral vision, and we zoomed down the last part of the hill. "Amazing, we're going to make it" I thought. Suddenly the right front wheel hit a small stone, just big enough to wrench the steering completely to the right. Mergatroid turned so sharply that Dan fell off—rolling and bouncing down the road, while I hung onto the steering ropes and rocketed over a small sidewalk, through a four foot high pricker-bush, carrying a large section of the bush with me on my head, and across the Baldwin sisters front lawn, digging ugly tire skid-trenches right up to the house. I stopped about three feet from the house. There in her living room window, which was open, was Miss Baldwin, who hated boys! She was screaming: "You filthy boys! Look what you've done to my hedge and my lawn. I'm calling the Police! You stay right there—don't you run away!"

Neither of us could run. Dan was lying in the road, trying to sit up, streaming blood from his arms, knees and head. Neither he nor I had any protective gear on—just shorts and T-shirts. I looked even worse, bleeding from the arms, head, neck and face where the pricker-bush had sliced me repeatedly. We were a mess.

I crawled then staggered out into the street to check on Dan, who was sitting up and listening to a man who was calling Dan every bad name in the book. The man was furious that we had almost caused him to run off the road into a tree. As I wobbled over to him and started to explain that the brake had failed, the angry man looked at me, bent over, and vomited. The cuts on my scalp were bleeding profusely, creating an effect that I was totally unaware of. Dan looked up at me and yelled: "You did that on purpose!" Then he punched me in the nose with his bloody hand. "I did not!" I yelled, and punched him back. And so we concluded our first, great mobile experiment in a fistfight.

Then the Police showed up and immediately started questioning the man, who had finally stopped vomiting, and they were blaming him for running us off of the road. Immediately Dan and I realized we had an opportunity to escape punishment…the age old "scape goat" had stumbled into the picture. We stopped fighting and said in unison: "That's right; he ran us off the road."

Unfortunately we forgot about the star witness: old Miss Baldwin, who had walked over to enter the scene of the crime. "Those filthy little boys did it all," she said. "I saw it with my own eyes—they have broken my window with a baseball, and Doctor Thurman's garage windows, and, and now they almost made that poor man run off the road into a tree!"

One of the Policemen asked us: "Where do you boys live?"

"Right next door," we pointed past Miss Baldwin's house.

This was true. Our back yard and the Baldwin sisters' back yard abutted, and we had hit a baseball through her dining room window…but only once. We had changed our backyard game by substituting a bristly push-broom for the baseball bat, which actually changed two things: we could no longer hit home runs through her windows, and the game was now called "brushball."

And so the police escorted Dan and me through the Baldwin back yard and into the Wilkinson back yard where we were given the truly uncomfortable option of telling Mother all or being taken to the Police Station and having Dad bail us out. We chose the "Mother option," knowing that she would not freak out at the sight of our considerably bloody bodies, because she was used to seeing us in that condition, and she would dress the cuts. It would be painful, because Mother used Methylate on all cuts—a tincture that stung more painfully than the cut itself. And we had learned that Mother was really good at enduring great pain as long as it was not her pain…

"Come on, don't be such a baby, this will only hurt for a little while." And, as always, she was right.

Dan and I were forced to retire Mergatroid; we were forbidden any playing in the street; we had to fix and replant the Baldwin's lawn, and we paid to replace their killer pricker-bush, and apologized profusely to the Baldwins, whom we thereafter referred to as "The Witches," and we never learned who the "Man" was that vomited in the street. And to this day, Dan still insists that I swerved on purpose to knock him off Murgatroid. All things considered, it was a spectacularly successful adventure.

THE TOYS

Rs Wilkinson

Bobby & Danny with plane

Toys in the 1940's and 1950's took patience. Almost nothing was preassembled. There were few instantly usable toys. There was no plastic. There were no battery powered toys, no computers, cellphones, computer games, etc. There was no superglue. There were detailed building plans for some toys: model airplanes, Erector Sets., Chemistry sets, Radio Shack kits. The airplane kits took many hours to assemble. It was not unusual to spend one or two months—fifty to one hundred actual building hours—many weekends and after school rainy days to assemble an airplane. I am not talking about a rubber band powered model. We built real gasoline engine powered planes.

Many of the neighborhood kids including: Bobby Stein brother Dan, and I, spent hours learning this skill. This was not a world of hyperactive kids. In fact I don't recall one hyperactive boy in school—grade or high school. Patience was quietly forced upon us because everything took time. Nothing clipped together; even Erector Sets were assembled with nuts and bolts and had detailed plans to follow.

The model planes took the longest to build but were the fastest in action. They came with sheets of "plans". The parts, various lengths and shapes and sticks of balsa wood which had to be cut to length or shape with an Exacto-knife, were then pinned using common pins, to a cardboard surface on which was the "plan". Then piece by piece they were glued together with a "fast-drying" glue which took at least thirty minutes to set. The models were gasoline engine powered, with miniature ignition systems, very similar to those used in automobiles...employing tiny spark plugs, condensers, points, and gas tanks. These motors were very difficult to start. Our right hand, index and middle fingers, were constantly bandaged because starting required the propeller to be rotated or spun counter clockwise by hand, quickly, because when the motor started, the propeller would spin and hit anything in its way, which was, of course, the fingers of our right hand. The miniature airplane props were sharp, and when learning this skill we often had bloody fingers. This was really training on how to be a man. I never saw a girl even try to start one of these engines. I was fairly sure that after watching us hop around in pain using all of the bad words we knew (which were precious few actually) that any self-respecting girl would consider herself seriously stupid for even trying such a pain inflicting, dumb activity. As boys, we considered ignoring pain and fear and shrugging at the sight of blood to be highly admirable traits and necessary for the advancement from little boy to big boy.

Bobby Stein and Dan and I became "experts" in the art of starting airplane engines. We were truly encouraged by the invention of the "glow plug." Glow plugs replaced the spark plug and all of the related ignition system (condensers, points, spark plugs) and made starting the engines much easier and predictable but no less dangerous to fingers. It still took many, often fifty or more, attempts to start one of the stubborn single cylinder power plants.

We all had small stands, clamped to tables, which held the motors stationary and enabled "test" runs. These were usually held in basements and lead to death threats and banishments by our mothers due to the god-awful noise and dangerous foul-smelling exhaust fumes which would permeate the house.

The actual flying of a plane took at least three people. One boy held the airplane, a second started the engine and a third boy, the pilot, stood fifty feet away, holding the control wires. The rudder on the tail of the plane was permanently glued at an angle which would keep the plane turning hard left. This was necessary because the models flew in a circle and were controlled by two fifty foot long wires which were attached to a six inch long handle which the pilot held at arm's length. The pilot had to turn in a circle to keep facing the plane as it flew. The handle with attached wires, kept the plane flying in a circle and controlled ailerons which made the plane climb or dive depending upon how the handle was held. Tilting the handle up made the plane climb—tilting down caused it to dive or nose down. And the planes were supposed to fly around and around in a circle until they ran out of gasoline—usually about five or six minutes, which was enough to make the pilot so dizzy that he often fell over…sometimes before the plane ran out of gas—which was disastrous. Crashing a plane after so many hours of preparation would have sent the lesser-hardened modern boy raised on instant gratification to at least three therapists if not the looney bin. However, we, raised on stupidity and stubbornness, simply dragged the mess home and got out the glue.

Occasionally, and we all accepted this as part of the game, the crash was terminal. Forever imprinted in my memory was the maiden flight of Bobby Stein's impressively beautiful model. The plane was large with about a three foot wingspan. A delicate framework: hundreds of carefully cut and glued pieces of balsa wood made the skeleton of hollow wings and fuselage over which was stretched model airplane ultra-thin paper, which was coated with airplane "dope," a water and gasoline resistant special paint. It was beautiful. The engines came in many sizes, and this model had a large one, designed to fly at about sixty miles per hour. We assembled the group of expert flyers at Butler Field, Province Lake, New Hampshire. A perfect, level field, surrounded by pine trees which kept out the occasional breeze...an ideal place to test the hundred hours of careful construction. Dan and I started and the held Bobby's plane, and at Bobby's signal, launched it into the air. If flew beautifully around in a circle, but just as it started its second revolution, an unexpected, strong, gust of wind blew across the field. The plane blew in towards Bobby, who back-pedaled frantically, trying to keep the control lines taught, but no, the plane swooped up into a steep climb, and then, reaching the end of the control lines, it was jerked back into a steep dive. The model powered straight down and into the ground, disintegrating into a sad pile of broken pieces. Horror, dismay, disbelief and despair registered on Bobby's face. We were in shock. Bobby was disconsolate—inconsolable. It was a total loss.

There was only one thing for it, I thought. "We need to destroy one of ours, to cheer Bobby up," I whispered to Dan .

"Get the 410 shotgun," Dan suggested.

"Beautiful," I said.

Brother Dan was the expert at long flying times—once keeping a plane in the air for ten minutes, and the only after effect that we noticed was that he listed to the right and kept making little right hand spin-arounds for several days. Once becoming experts at starting and flying these models we, as all-American normal boys, naturally progressed to the art of destroying them. Dan, who was our demolition expert, partly through skill and partly clumsiness, had come up with the supreme destruction idea.

"I'll gas up my long-flying model and you can shoot at it with the shotgun."

Bobby was still looking at his wrecked plane, slowly shaking his head. It was going to be hard to cheer him up. We convinced him to walk to the "upper field," about a half-mile up the road, and I retrieved my gun from our house. The weapon was a double barrel, single shot 22 rifle and 410 shotgun "over and under." This meant that the 22 rifle was the top barrel and the 410 shotgun, which is a very small gauge or size, was the bottom barrel of the gun. I had been given this gun at the age of twelve, which in those days was the age of responsibility—which meant that I would be held accountable for any misuse of the weapon. Use of the gun was restricted to shooting tin cans, porcupines (which chewed through two-by-eight floor joists under the house) rats at the town dump, and targets. Even unloaded guns were never aimed at or in the direction of a person, and we were all trained in the correct usage of them. This was a non-approved usage of dangerous materials. We were running the risk of parental disapproval and discipline—a respect that prevented many disasters. However compared to the dangers associated with drugs, the internet, pornography, kidnapping, pedophiles and terrorists, which were never even discussed in our world in the '40's and 50's, and are common now, we were comfortably safe and lucky.

And so I loaded up the shotgun, stood ready to fire at Dan's beautiful, small (about 14 inch wingspan) model airplane, as it flew by. I was using number six birdshot. No one expected me to hit the plane, but I did know how to shoot at and lead a moving target because I had shot at and hit clay pigeons, which were really just clay discs that were propelled through the air for target practice. Bobby started the engine, I launched the model, and Dan was the pilot. I picked up the gun, waited for the second pass over head, aimed, and BOOM—a direct hit! We were astonished as the plane disintegrated in mid-air!

"Sensational," exclaimed Bobby.

"Good one," said Dan, "a complete destruction! My plane is totally useless!!"

Bobby and Dan were cheering, laughing, and slapping each other on the back

It was so good to see Bobby smiling…this day WAS a success after all.

DAVE'S CANOE

RS Wilkinson

In 1947 Dave was 16 years old. Although we sometimes played back-yard games with Dave, Dan and I were considered too young to be involved in our older brothers or sister's activities. This was as it should be. We were tattletales mainly because we were jealous. Older kids whispered about things they did, and they specifically uninvited us to participate…they did not trust us.

For instance, take sex. Ever since we first discovered (certainly by age five) that out little "hosers" were physically pleasurable play-things, we were very interested in sex. We did not talk about this in front of adults…ever! They and we pretended that sexual attraction did not exist. "It" was never mentioned in front of any adult including my nine years older brother, Sam, (who was called Allen until he was twenty-five) or my seven years older sister, Peggy. Fortunately we could talk about anything with Dave—we figured he knew everything—but he would not include us in his great knowledge of women because he knew we could not handle the truth. Of course he was right about this. "Handling" something really meant keeping your mouth shut which was apparently something that one learned only through experience—which we did not have.

Dave did not have a canoe. This story is not really about a canoe or about being in a canoe, but it is about sex and being under a canoe…

which in my opinion is the best possible use of canoes. It started on the beach of Province Lake, NH. It was dusk. Summertime. A warm sunset had just wrapped up a fun day on the beach. Dave was talking with a truly beautiful girl, Rose. She was not at all interested in me or my younger brother, Danny, but she and Dave had locked eyes. Dave told Danny and me to go home. I knew he was trying to get rid of us, and I was jealous and angry about being excluded. So… Danny and I pretended to head for home, but actually hid in the bushes that lined the edge of the beach and waited quietly hoping to see something forbidden or at least informational. Dave did not disappoint. Within five minutes he had progressed from holding Rose's hand to actually kissing her on the lips. We had never seen this before (remember this was 1947 and even the movies we were allowed to watch, which were always Westerns, rarely had any kissing, plus they were always goodbye kisses as the hero rode off into the sunset). This was spectacularly different. Dave and Rose actually seemed to like kissing, and they were not doing it right…Danny and I noticed that it was not at all like the way Mother had taught us: pursed tight lips for a microsecond of contact. No, they seemed to be mashing their mouths together, twisting their heads side to side…and they must have been in pain because they were both moaning loudly enough so that we could hear them from our hiding observation spot.

"This is awful!" observed Danny, "I think they need help."

"Wait, Sshhhh See, they're crawling under that upside-down canoe on the beach. Oh, this is going to be good!"

Danny frowned, "Why is it so good? Look, Dave's trying to smother her, and oh, oh, look out!"

The canoe had been propped up with a stick which held one side up far enough off of the beach so that Dave and Rose could crawl under it. But Dave's leg suddenly spasmed out, kicking the stick away and allowing the canoe to close over them. The canoe gave several small humps as if it were attempting to rise up and then settled down onto the sand.

"They need help! They're dying!" said Danny. "Let's get Dad."

And so we both turned and ran as fast as we could—one half mile, straight up Province Mountain through a path in the woods we had made from the beach to our house. It was getting really dark, and we kept running into branches and stumbling over roots wishing we had a flashlight. We were used to walking the road at night, but the path was a challenge. Dad was sitting on the porch enjoying a quiet evening when we burst through the screen door, totally out of breath and taking turns gasping: "Dave is, huff, is dying, huff, under a canoe, huff-huff, with Rose, huff-huff, and, and huff, hurt bad!!… and, huff, huff, Rose was moaning and kissing Dave, huff, huff, but she needs help to save him!"

Instantly Dad was on his feet asking us: "Where is he? What canoe? How deep is the water?"

And this great sinking feeling hit my stomach…Dad thinks they are drowning. Maybe, just maybe I am the one who is in trouble.

I try to say helpfully: "They are not in the water, ahh, they're on the beach—where we usually go."

"On the beach? Get in the car. Show me where they are."

And so I rode down the mountain with Dad and Danny, trying to think of something to say, knowing that everyone was in trouble and it was my fault. Danny said nothing, he had figured out that silence was the best policy.

When we reached the lake, Dad drove along the beachfront road until we saw the still overturned canoe, and he turned left off of the road until his headlights lit up the love-nest. While we cowered in the car, staring through the front windshield, we watched Dad running to the canoe and lifting up one side and heaving it over and off of the now terrified couple.

Dave scrambled from his knees to a wobbly standing position while trying to shade his eyes from the blinding headlights. Then he turned away and fumbled with his pants, trying to tuck in his shirt. Rose, a mess of sandy hair, was shakily fastening her blouse but getting the buttons all misaligned as she turned away from the lights. She kept looking up and down and then just stood there, turned again and faced Dad. I was flooded with respect and passion for her. She raised her head and stared directly at Dad.

"What were you two doing?...never mind! Don't ever let me catch you doing that again...well, speak up!" Dad seemed strangely unable to make sense—very unusual for him.

Dave finally started, "We were ahhh...Rose was showing me how to find the Big Dipper in the sky (the stars were beautiful by now) and we just sort-of rolled under the canoe by mistake. Good thing you came by to save us. As you can see, we were struggling to get out from under that thing!"

My admiration for Dave's composure under fire was mightily reinforced. I was in awe. He was actually saying this stuff with a straight face, and Rose was somberly nodding in agreement.

Dad's face seemed to turn red, even in the car's headlights. Then the veins on his neck swelled up, and finally he could not hold it in any longer and he started shaking with laughter...the pent-up relief of a father discovering that his son was not drowning but merely "discovering" the Big Dipper!

Rose was sent home, immediately, to her camp which was about three hundred feet away. Dave was ordered to walk up the road behind the car. We drove in a slow silence until Dad said: "We will not tell anybody about this. Do you understand? Anybody. Ever. Not your brother, your sister or your Mother!"

We both nodded emphatically in the darkness of the back seat in the car. Somehow Danny and I realized that this was one of the extremely important differences between men and women.

Dan and I kept the secret of our betrayal of Dave for 32 years. Feeling strong guilt about my tattletale role in this event, which I also felt had given him The Black Cloak for good; I finally confessed to Dave that Dan and I had ratted him out, and that was how Dad knew Dave was under the canoe. Dave looked at me in surprise, then smiled and said. "I can't recall that Dad ever gave me the Black Cloak...but just in case, that is exactly why I always tried to leave you behind..."

Unfortunately my Brother left us behind forever in 1983, but I am sure that Dave often again located the Big Dipper, and every time I look up to the Northern stars in the evening I smile and see him there.

THE BICYCLE

RS Wilkinson

"Dad, there is a Schwinn bike for sale…it's cheap. It is a really good buy—in great shape…and it is right down the street at the Beckwith's…Jimmy says he'll sell it to me for fifteen dollars. Could I possibly get it as an early birthday present?"

I would be fourteen on May fifth—it was March first, 1949.

Dad was quiet for a minute and said, "No."

"Well, how about an early birthday and Christmas present combined? It has only one gear—high gear…so it is fast on the level and going downhill. I could probably beat Bobby Stein in a race."

This logic seemed impeccably sound to me, but Dad said "No" again.

"Could you loan me the money? You could take it out of my allowance." I was paid, twenty-five cents a week for: washing and drying dishes, setting the table, serving food, clearing the table for five of us kids, our parents and grandmother, eight people, and taking out the trash, which included emptying the ashes and clinkers from our coal furnace into as many as seven 35 gallon steel cans and carrying them up a flight of cement stairs—often ice coated in the winter—down the side of the house along a sixty foot sidewalk, then down a flight of cement stairs to the street, and line them up off of the sidewalk on the edge of the street. The cans weighed about sixty

46

pounds when filled with ash, and they were taken out on Sunday and returned to the basement on Monday.

Our house was a heating challenge: three stories, nine bedrooms, all wood, built in 1900, and the huge, hungry hot-air coal furnace with no fan, just convection, needed tending every ten hours or so, which meant shaking down the "clinkers" (dying lumps of mostly burned coal) using a huge crank that inserted into the grates and shaking back and forth, a motion requiring all of my strength, to shake the ash until if fell into the clean-out compartment in the bottom of the furnace. Then we flung six to eight shovelfuls of coal into the furnace on top of the bed of glowing coals…opened up the draft to get the coal burning, waited ten minutes, and closed the draft down. Then, we, Dave, my older brother, and later Dan, who was three years younger than I, took turns shoveling out the ashes into the metal barrels. Finally, we helped each other drag them up the basement stairs, which was no fun, developed impressive muscles and greatly increased our ability to swear.

There were other jobs too: appearing in the kitchen by 6:45 AM to help prepare breakfast, which included hand-squeezing ten oranges for juice, and setting the table for eight. There were five of us children, and we all helped with specific jobs or no allowance. No questions and no complaints were allowed.

This gave all of us a precious, and now treasured, feeling of worth, participation and responsibility—much of which is regrettably lacking today. But I had no bike, and at twenty-five cents a week, it looked almost hopeless.

I looked at Dad and mustered up one last question/statement: "I guess that means no bike."

"You could get a job and buy It." said Dad, softly.

"Like, what job??"

"Mowing lawns, taking out trash, delivering papers."

So I knew what I was worth—my areas of expertise were defined—and I also knew that fifteen dollars was a lot of money (at least two hundred in 2015 dollars).

The next day I walked down to Cleveland Circle to apply for a paper route… "OK kid, where's your bike? We'll put a basket on it."

"I need to save the money to buy the bike," I said.

"Right, Kid. So, a walking route? You might earn five cents a day."

"I'll take it, better than I get with my current job."

"Jeez, Kid, what kind of work you doing?"

"Well, hauling out coal ashes and stuff…"

"Where you live, Kid?"

"292 Clinton Rd."

"NO shit?? Clinton Rd.??"

Adults never swore in front of kids…I knew what shit was, but we only used the word on the playground, NEVER in front of adults—so I was truly impressed.

"No shit, I replied," trying to act like a big kid.

"Hey, kid, we don't use that kind of language around here unless you're a grownup—how old are you anyway?"

"Sixteen," I lied.

"OK, I'll give you a bag to hold the papers. You start on Clark Rd.—I'll give you the house numbers tomorrow—be here at 6AM"

And so, I had my first job.

I knew where Clark Rd. was, it ran parallel to Clinton Rd. No problem…except for the two dogs who tried to bite me until Mr. Bumblethorp yelled at them to leave me alone, and Mrs. Bumblethorp, who invited me in on Saturdays, saying that her husband was away on business and she needed help with her sink faucet which was dripping. I remember her clearly: she always had a sheer nightie on…the kind you could almost see through, a sort-of pale pink that clung to her breasts and her nipples in a fascinating way that gave me an instant and noticeable erection even though I leaned over like I had a stomach ache to try to hide it. The first week I left as quickly as I could, saying I had a lot of papers to deliver. The second week I stayed for coffee—hiding my erection under the table as best I could. The third week she asked me what I was hiding under the table, and too inexperienced and embarrassed to answer intelligently, I said:"Nothing."

"Well", Mrs. Bumblethorp said: "Bobby, that is not nothing!"

And so, I learned that low wages can have non-taxable benefits.

I also told her of my financial dilemma and need for a bike, and she graciously offered to augment my income by hiring me to take out her trash at the wage of one dollar a week. I thought it doesn't get better than this!!

Dad asked how the job was going, and how long it would take to save up for the bike, and I told him that my walking paper route would probably take months…maybe a year to save the fifteen dollars!

Actually I had the money and the bike on the first of June, four months latter! It was a great day, and I was really excited and proud, and happy to show off my purchase to Dad, who was also impressed that I had saved the money so quickly. But there is more to this story: my younger brother, Dan, had received a new English Raleigh bike—the only bike which shifted with three speeds—for Christmas that year. He had earned the bike by keeping his grades up. I had not worked such a deal nor was I interested in keeping my grades up because I was a "selective" performer at school: meaning that I did well if I was interested in the subject matter and liked the teacher. Thus, the bike situation was really of my own doing…but I was still angry at my Dad for what I thought was the favoritism shown my younger brother. I looked proudly at the Schwinn, and Dad took me aside and said: " The lesson is that this is your bike. You earned it, you own it, and nobody, not even I can take it away or restrict your use of it…not for your behavior or grades." I got the point, I had bitter-sweet satisfaction, but still my younger brother had the far better bike…

MY DOGGY, WITH BOB STEIN

RS Wilkinson

Bobby Stein was a genius. I was a genius. IQ tests confirmed this. Bob and I were called "Bobby" until we grew up. Neither of us was handsome as a teenager. Bobby Stein was about 5'7" and I towered over him at 5'8". He was my best friend, living across the street and three houses away.

Two geniuses, fifteen year old boys doing stuff together that was interesting and dangerous. The interesting part we both got, but the dangerous part...to that we were oblivious. And we were creative. I thought I could play the guitar and become a famous Country/ Western singer. Bobby would be the production manager/promoter/ engineer/radio announcer/recording studio operator/ and the builder of the transmitter. That's right—transmitter.

Radio Shack had just opened its first Boston store and Bobby said we could find the parts to make a "really powerful transmitter" by buying a kit that would build a radio (a receiver) and then modifying the receiver to make it into a transmitter. We were not supposed to do this, we knew, because the FCC, whatever that was, said it was illegal, but we also reasoned that we were totally unknown and they would never find us. The power of transmitters was measured in WATTS, and we also believed that if we kept the wattage down, whatever we broadcast would only be heard on radios in our immediate neighborhood. So, a very weak transmitter would be OK…never even picked up by the FCC.

Bobby and I worked to build the transmitter, but I must say that I only helped with the soldering and connecting of the parts. Bobby was the brains behind this one. My real contribution was the music: a wonderful, sophisticated song that I wrote and performed, playing guitar and singing, entitled MY DOGGY AND ME. The astounding lyrics were:

"My doggy, my doggy, my doggy and me, my doggy had a flea, it bit him on the knee.

My doggy, my doggy, my doggy and me, little doggy won't you please come home and stay with me?

He left me on one sunny day, I didn't see him to this day, little doggy why'd you ever go away, what a fool you made of yourself that day.

My doggy, my doggy, my doggy and me, little doggy won't you please come home and stay with me?

My doggy, my doggy, my doggy bit his flea, he also bit his knee, he also bit his knee,

My doggy, my doggy, he died the other day, now little doggy can never come with me to stay.

He left me on one sunny day, little doggy why'd you ever go away? What a fool you made of yourself that day, now little doggy can never come with me to stay.

He left me on one sunny day—little doggy why'd you ever go away?

What a fool you made of yourself that day, little doggy won't you please come home with me to stay?"

Obviously a truly touching song with a great, heart-rending, tear jerking set of lyrics in the finest old country tradition.

We spent two days and several rehearsals carefully preparing for the first broadcast, and Bobby Stein's brilliant introduction included: "done on DEKKA records, by Robert Wilkinson, an entirely unknown songwriter." He also had used my real name and cleverly identified himself as "Jim Barrows of the Hillbilly Bandstand," a complete fabrication.

There is more, and it gets even better: Bobby had…and I cannot recall from where, managed the loan of a record cutting machine. That's right, it would "cut" a real wax recording on a small, 78 rpm disc of hard, brittle plastic. We made a record which lasted about four minutes, of our "radio broadcast," complete with Bobby apologizing for his lisping because he had just been to the dentist (which was true,) and his introducing me, and, of course, my singing the great My Doggy Song, which he predicted was sure to become a "top ten" hit. We even did a " lead-in" thirty second clip featuring a real country singer, which opened our performance and was followed by Bobby's intro, then my singing and finally whistling the tune of "By the Light of the Silvery Moon. " We had to cut both sides of the record because on the first try we both lost it and started laughing uncontrollably. We still have both originals of this priceless work of geniuses.

Bobby had rigged up a long antenna on his garage, and he had added capacitors and resistors and condensers to the circuitry to boost up the power, because we wanted my brother, Dave, to listen on Dad's car radio at our house, which was about 800 feet away. The radio frequency we chose was the same as WHDH—a major station in the Boston area.

Our first broadcast was done at noon on Saturday, and Dave, who had listened on the car radio, reported that it came in fine. A little too fine—it had come in clearly in the car almost down to Kenmore square. In other words, we had covered most of the 50,000 people in Brookline. "So strong that it blanked out HDH (as we called it) completely and replaced "Bob and Ray," a well know popular comedy, radio show. Dave also informed us that almost immediately after we went off the air, the announcer in downtown Boston said: "What the heck was that? We apologize for that astounding interruption!" Then with all of us tuned into HDH, we heard the announcer say: "We have received many calls regarding that…whatever it was…interruption, and most listeners said it was the funniest thing they have ever heard and couldn't wait for the next one." Well, in spite of the fact that the announcer said NOT to interrupt his programming again, we interpreted his reaction our way: as far as we were concerned we were a smash hit! Bobby's transmitter was putting out truly impressive wattage!

So we decided an expanded broadcast was in order. Our second broadcast was carefully planned for 5:15 PM on Monday—rush hour traffic at its peak in the Boston area seemed a good time to reach the most people. Remember that this was before television—almost everybody would be at home or driving and listening to radio news. We were sure we would be famous, maybe getting our own radio show: "The Bob and Bob Show" with the Doggy Song as its theme. We congratulated each other on a sensational job of ensuring our successful future. And then, about two minutes after concluding the great performance…we heard the screeching of brakes in the driveway. The front door of the house SLAMMED! The clomping of feet coming down the stairs into the basement, which was our construction and broadcast room, and BOOM! Bobby Stein's father burst into the room.

"I JUST HEARD YOU GODDAMN IDIOTS ON THE CAR RADIO!! WHERE IS THAT TRANSMITTER? YOU'RE GOING TO GET US ALL ARRESTED!"

He spotted the transmitter sitting on our "workbench," a small table in the middle of the room, and raised our little gem over his head and flung it down onto the cement basement floor—smashing it "to smithereens." I immediately concluded that the ecstasy of victory had turned into the agony of defeat and raced for the stairs, and not daring to say a word, ran out the front door and almost into Dave, who was driving Dad's car with a big smile on his face. I jumped into the car, and Dave said that we were an even bigger success this time, that: "The radio announcer had just said that some guy from the Federal government wanted to talk to us," and Dave figured that they wanted to hire us because we were so funny!

This brought several potential projects that Bobby and I had planned to a halt, mostly because I did not feel exactly welcome at his house for a while. Bobby went on to graduate from MIT, became a chief executive at Raytheon, and a highly respected leader in the town of Brookline. Finally, thanks to my daughter, who found the original record in a pile of our old "junk," and brother, Dan, who made extra copies, we have a digital copy and a CD of the original recording of the Doggy song broadcast. My friendship with Bobby Stein, which endures today, even survived more joint ventures…one involving tennis, and our previous painful experience with model airplanes.

THE BLACK CLOAK:
IN MEMORY OF DAVE AND
DAVE'S CHRISTMAS TREE

RS Wilkinson

Dave's Christmas Tree

Dave was 18 in 1948…he could drive; he even had a license, but he usually did not take me with him. I was too young, and no older brother wanted a younger brother tagging along. Mother included me against Dave's protests: "Go down to Cleveland Circle and buy a Christmas tree. I am giving you ten dollars to do this, so be sure you pick out a good one, and bring back any change…and take Bobby with you to help with tying the tree on top of the car, (which also silently implied that I would tell on him if Dave improvised on her plan)…and be careful, don't scratch the car." The car was Dad's 1947 Desoto, which had survived "The 360" and several more of Mother's near-death driver-learning experiences. The warning from Mother was aimed at Dave, the usual wearer of the Black Cloak. Dave and I were often the troublemakers…into, and sometimes out of, mischief related punishments for crimes of which we might have been guilty, but occasionally were innocent and looked guilty. We often swapped wearing the figurative cloak, and early-on learned that just looking guilty was enough proof to cause the "Black Cloak of Guilt" to be assigned. We also knew that the cloak of guilt could be assigned to a completely innocent bystander…especially by our Mother, who was justifiably suspicious, untrusting, constantly looking for deception and assigning by insinuation or direct accusation, the blame. Nobody was exempt from Mother's accusing eye, even Dad, but Dave and I practically owned the Cloak.

Dave was with me when the latest of these blame transferals had occurred in October on a Sunday drive on Rt. 25 in New Hampshire when Mother decided to learn how to pass another car. We, Dave, Dan and I, were riding in the back seat. We were following a slow-moving farm truck when suddenly Mother lurched to her left, leaning her head against the window and turning the wheel to the left. The car, not known for its nifty handling, wallowed into the left lane. I sighed in relief because sitting behind Mother, I could see that there was no oncoming car. There were no horns blowing. I could hear out of my open back window—I thought we were safe. But no. Dad loudly said: "Margaret, what are you doing? Pull over."

"I'm passing."

"Pull over"

Mother swerved more to the left. Incredibly, Mother had chosen to pass on a bridge—an old bridge with steel girders that rose up about fifteen feet along both sides. Dad wanted her to pull back in line, but Mother thought he meant for her to pull further out to pass. Mother stomped on the gas and the old Fluid Drive down shifted, the engine roared, the car slowly, as if pulled by a rubber band, accelerated. Then I heard it: we were so close to the girders that they made a SHWIKOOO, SHWIKKOO, SHWIKOOO sound as they passed my window. Dad grabbed for the wheel. I closed my eyes, waiting for the crash. It seemed a long, long time…then I peeked ahead. Miraculously we had passed the truck and survived again… the bridge must have moved out of the way!

Dad was speechless. Mother felt the need to comment: "Well, I knew we could make it, there was nobody coming at us—and we were doing just fine until you told me to pull over…it was your fault" and she turned and glared at Dad.

I had the shakes…"We need to take extra underwear when Mother drives, " I whispered to Dave

He nodded, eyes wide open in amazement, and whispered: "She just gave the Black Cloak to Dad!".

So, when Mother sent us to buy a Christmas tree and said: "Be careful" to Dave, who was a skillful driver, I bit my tongue in silence. Disrespect or verbal criticism of adults was not allowed. Dave reassured Mother that all would be well with this venture, and I nodded in agreement…excited that I was going unchaperoned.

Cleveland Circle was only about a mile from our house. It was a traffic circle on Beacon Street, with several stores and restaurants lining the area. The Christmas trees were leaning against the wall of a small market, and because it was December 24, there were not many trees left from which to choose. We had not bought a tree earlier because Mother felt that Christmas should be celebrated on Christmas day and not before. This meant buying the tree and decorating it and the house on Christmas Eve. This was fine with all of us because it made Christmas really special. However, on this particular year, it made finding a good tree nearly impossible, and Dave's wonderful, mischievous nature turned the mundane chore into an exciting adventure.

We looked at the sorry display of left-over trees. There was one good one left, priced at ten dollars, which we did have. But Dave noticed a liquor store right next to the Christmas tree pile, and he instructed me to wait until he went into the store to get some change…this he justified by noting that most of the trees were marked down to five dollars. Ten minutes later he emerged with five dollars in one hand and a brown paper bag in his other hand.

"What is that?" I asked. Dave smiled. ..imagine the BEST smile you have ever seen, and that was Dave.

He held up a bottle labeled: Jack Daniels. Then he put his index finger across his lips and whispered: "Don't tell anyone."

I was so happy to be included in the "big boy" world that I instantly swore allegiance to the secret.

"What is it for?"

"I have a date," he said.

"Does she drink?

"She does."

"Can I go too?" I knew this was a hopeless question.

"No, come on, let's get the tree. Try to pick out the best look-ing one."

The trees were pitiful—full of short limbs with huge gaps—just open space, and the needles had already dropped off of the bot-tom limbs which sagged miserably down.

Dave grabbed one of the five dollar trees, and said: "This one will do fine if we put one side up against the wall so no one can see it."

"But it always goes in front of the windows. They'll see right through it," I complained.

"We always put it up at night—don't turn on the lights until we get stuff put on it, and close the blinds behind it. Nobody will notice until after we get our presents." Dave nodded, and, a small, reassuring smile flickered for an instant.

And so we tied the tree on top of the car, stripping most of the remaining needles off in the process, and drove home to be met by my brother Dan.

Dan, who was three years younger than I, took one look at it when we got it home and sadly observed that it needed lots of stuff hung on it, so he went upstairs to get the boxes of ornaments which were stored in a closet on the third floor. I was standing at the foot of the stairs as Dan started down. He had two big boxes, full of balls and lights and other breakable ornaments. I sensed trouble because Dan had the reputation of being clumsy, and sure enough he stepped out into space off of the top step and exclaimed, "OH NO!" It was a world class, eggbeater style, stairway descention, as he clutched at the railing spindles, breaking several of them while trying to stop himself, rolling over and over, making loud groans and grunts and finally ending up on top of the boxes at the bottom of the stairs, having destroyed at least half of our ornaments in the process.

Mother was in the kitchen, and asked "What was that?" I was laughing so hard I could not talk. Then Mother appeared, saw Dan at the bottom of the stairs, tangled up in a mess of broken ornaments and stair spindles, pretending to be mortally wounded, and she turned to me and said:" Shame on you, laughing at your brother who just fell down stairs. You go to your room and wait there until your Father comes home!"

One hour later, alone, sitting in my room, I heard a small knock. We were all brought up to knock on anyone's door and wait for an answer before entering. I asked: "Who is it?"

"It's Dave, can I come in?"

"Yes," I said.

Dave came in hiding the bottle of Bourbon under his shirt. "Here…we are both members of the Black Cloak Club…take a sip, brother."

It wasn't the liquor that warmed my heart. I had been accepted.

I chanced asking Dave a question: "Why do all girls, old and young, like you so much? You get A's from your teachers and don't even do the homework."

Dave looked at me, deciding if I were old enough to hear this important information, then he said: "Three things…always tell girls you like their dress or hair, use big words, and most important is how you say them."

"How you say them?"

"Yup, smile and mean what you say."

"But you once told a girl she looked 'especially cadaverous' and she still liked you."

"Yup," he nodded seriously, "because I said it right. You have to look into their eyes too. "

This may have been the best advice I ever received. And I still remember this as the best Christmas I ever had. Dave and I continued our special kinship over the years…often swapping the Black Cloak. Neither of us focused our energy on making money or on living up to someone else's expectations.

And that is how we wound up with the worst excuse for a Christmas tree that I have ever seen. It was truly an embarrassment. There were almost no branches. We hung every light, piece of tinsel, ball, ornament…even whipped up ivory soap flakes into a gooey mess thinking it would look like snow, and covered the scrawny branches, but the tree looked like a dead, wet rat.

Mother was not happy. Dad was not happy. Dad came in and took a picture of "it" before we could finish "decorating" it, and suggested that we pile the presents under the bottom limbs to prop them up. Older sister, Peg, said it would make us a "laughing stock," whatever that was. Oldest brother, Sam just shook his head sadly… and Bobby Stein, my best friend, said: "I am glad we don't have one of those in our house." At this point we envied the small size and economic efficiency of the Menorah.

Finally, alone with Dave and Jack Daniels, I asked Dave how, at only eighteen, could he buy liquor in Massachusetts? I knew we had to be twenty-one to drink or buy liquor. He did not look old enough. He was five foot seven inches tall. He did not have a deep voice…no way could he pass for twenty one.

Dave smiled, looked at me, and said: "There was a girl helping people in the liquor store. Her father owns the liquor store." Then he smiled again and said…"She's my date."

BOBBY STEIN AND THE LONGWOOD CRICKET CLUB TENNIS MATCH

RS Wilkinson

Bobby Stein

1951 was a big year for me because I was sixteen. I didn't look sixteen. When I went for my driver's license exam, the inspecting officer asked me if I were really sixteen…three times. So, even though I looked about twelve—no need to rub it in. The guy even checked my birth certificate again as he handed me my temporary license.

Any respect at that age had to be earned, but I had learned the hard way that it was important to keep my mouth shut when in the presence of authority figures—especially if they actually had authority. Hence I meekly and thankfully accepted the license. I was pretty fed up with faking respect—a personality trait which often produced dismal results.

On the Dean Road Playground we did have respect if we produced, which meant that our games were fiercely contested winning-oriented battles. Bobby Stein was an incredible athlete. Neither he nor I possessed the athlete's body. We were both short, and as my grade school teacher observed: "built close to the ground." I was a fast runner, but Bobby could beat me at running from my house to his, a distance of about 800 feet. In football he would kick off and the ball would always get to the end zone. I clearly remember our team's smirks turning into astonishment when he dropkicked extra points and field-goals. In high school we went to different schools. I went to B&N, Bobby was at Roxbury Latin. In our senior year we played against each other. We lost, and Bobby was the star player on the field.

But this story is not about football. During the spring of 1951 Bobby had been playing tennis. He played and practiced on the tarred, free courts of the Dean Rd. Playground, where a ragged assortment of kids floundered back and forth sporting old wooden, often warped, tennis racquets, whacking awkwardly at the old, beat-up tennis balls which were often found lying around the courts. He might also have practiced at school, but I didn't know about that. So when he told me he had entered the New England Junior Tennis Tournament, it meant nothing to me. After all, I was a wrestler and football player.

"It will be held at the Longwood Cricket Club, and I need someone to go with me to help watch my stuff while I'm playing and to help me get warmed-up. It is this coming Saturday. Will you go with me?"

"Well, OK," I said, "except I don't know about the warming-up stuff. I can hardly get the ball over the net."

I had "played" twice with Bobby. I hardly knew how to keep score. All I was capable of was lobbing the ball over to him, and then only if it was an easy return shot. Bobby was strong, and once he really hit the ball—it struck me and hurt, so I told him to: "Cut that stuff out!" As a result, I agreed that I would just warm him up if he took it easy on me.

And so he did.

When we arrived at the Club I knew I had made a big mistake. This was a club for millionaires. They had pristine grass courts. Everything was so high-priced that I could not even afford a Coke. The players were all dressed in clean, pressed, white shirts and shorts and new tennis shoes. They were tall, lean, blond, mostly blue-eyed, sporting new racquets—some of them had beautiful girls carrying their spare racquets.

"Look at them," I whispered.

"Shhhhhsh," said Bobby.

They were staring at us and laughing. Bobby was dressed in old, worn-out, grubby sneakers with a grey T-shirt and grey cut-off baggy, raggedy sweat pants. I was in an old pair of faded blue shorts, blue sneakers, and a Mickey Mouse T-shirt.

Bobby said, "You go check in and see how I am seeded and who I am playing and when it actually starts. Then, when you come back, we'll get warmed up."

I started to feel sick to my stomach, but headed to a line of people who appeared to be signing in. When it was my turn, a man, sitting at a small table in a starched white uniform slowly looked me down and then up, leaning his head back so that what I could see clearly was up his nostrils, and slowly said: "eeeyes, are you a participant?"

I threw my head back to show him my nostrils and slowly said: "Possibly."

Long pause…"Possibly what?"

Long pause…"Stein. Robert Stein."

The nostrils lowered into reading position, and by leaning over I could read the chart of entrants and see that Bobby was seeded last, which meant he would play the first seeded or best player. They had never heard of Stein because he had never before entered any tournament.

"And might you be Mr. Stein?"

Long pause, "NOOO, I am Mr. Wilkinson, Mr. Stein's Manager."

"I see...Is Mr. Stein here and prepared to play? We shall commence the tournament at noon, sharp. I must tell you that If a participant is more than ten minutes late, it will result in forfeiture of the match."

I raised my chin until my neck hurt, opened my mouth slightly stretching the upper lip down over my teeth, raised my tongue to the top of my mouth and breathed sibilantly: "Yes, I must tell you that I feel confident Mr. Stein will be satisfactorily prepared at noon, provided that he has a practice court in good condition for the preparatory warm-up. Which court shall we employ?"

He looked at the chart on the table and said, "You are assigned court number 5, you may occupy it from 11:45 until noon." I noticed he had a name tag on, reading: T.T.B. Barrington.

"Thank you, Mr. Barington, much obliged, " I said, with as much dignity as I could muster.

I ran back to Bobby and reported the bad news: "You're playing the number one seed. I think that's him over on court number 4. He looks good. His name is James Harburton the Third! He hasn't lost a match this year. I have been watching him and I notice he often looks over your way, and he and his friends are making fun of you. I overheard him say, "this won't take long."

I started to feel sick to my stomach again.

Bobby looked over at the handsome group of Harburton admirers and observed: "Some of those girls look pretty good."

"Yeah, " I said, " And we don't stand a chance with them...they won't even talk with us."

"Yeah, I see that. Let's get warmed up," said Bobby.

And for fifteen minutes the crowd of Harburton supporters watched us as I struggled to return Bobby's lobs and he ran awkwardly back and forth, his baggy cut offs flapping around his tree trunk legs, lobbing the ball back to me. I also tried a few serves. Most of them were "out" anyway, but Bobby returned them all. Then we shook hands, and he gave me a big smile, and the observers clapped wildly, laughing and joking about what a spectacle we were.

Indeed we were a sorry spectacle. I couldn't blame them for laughing at us. Except for the minute of forced bravado when talking with TTB Barrington, I was embarrassed, actually ashamed of myself and the shoddy appearance we were making. I even had moments of blaming Bobby for getting me into this mess. We had no business being here. Nobody would respect or like us…we were what my Mother would call a "laughing stock". I guessed this expression came from when people were punished for crimes by putting them in "the stocks" in the town square.

However there were at least three things that I knew about Bobby: he was very fast, very strong and very smart. I also had faith in his service…I mean his tennis serve. It was a rocket—I had never been able to return it. I watched Bobby and the other boy shake hands. Harburton was poised, confident, elegant, handsome, impeccably attired. Bobby was, well, not any better to look at than I was, so I scrunched down trying to be invisible. Then the match started.

Bobby had first serve. The look on Harburton's face changed from bored, superior— I have to tolerate this?— to jaw-dropping amazement. The amazement turned to respect, then discouragement then utter defeat. Bobby won in straight sets. His serve was never returned—not once, and his volleys were overwhelming. He had beaten the unbeatable first seed so completely that by the end of the match everybody was gathered around the court. I was jumping up and down and cheering and at the end, almost everyone was cheering.

After the match Bobby was surrounded by good looking girls, and some of them even talked with me…after all, I was the "manager" and they wanted to know about the new tennis sensation: what was his name, where did he live, what was his telephone number? Unfortunately they did not want to talk about the importance of "managing." And they all said that after watching me warm up the champion, even they could beat me in tennis, and that they could do a much better job of warming up and managing than I. Ironically, I had apparently done such a superior job of "managing" that it was going to cost me my job! Several of the players went over to talk with Bobby, and even TTB Barrington suggested that we might be con-

sidered "eligible to apply" for membership if we met certain require-
ments—which I was pretty sure we did not.

Still, I was very excited by the prospect of managing a tennis
star, and encouraged Bobby, who had gone on to easily win the
entire tournament, to seriously continue competing in tennis, but
he declined because his goal was to enter MIT, which he did. I have
heard that he recently played tennis with a famous surgeon, a member of The Longwood Cricket Club, who was tall, good looking,
properly dressed, and thought, because he played several times a
week that he was pretty good at tennis. He confidently challenged
Bob (Bobby) to a match—I could have told him…big mistake!

THE SUBMARINE

RS Wilkinson

In 1951 Doc Walters was my eleventh grade Science teacher…my best teacher that year because he was the most interesting, by far. Doc asked all of us in his class to enter the Science Fair at the school. He wanted creative, interesting, science oriented projects. Right away I was stumped: He wanted a physical creation, not wild imagination, but the creation had to be "creative" right? Sure, very clear, so I actually gave the project some thought—like for two days. Finally the light went on in my brain. I mention this because I was usually "in my own world."

When I was nine years old, I knew that I was not a "good student". This I knew because it had been repeated many times by my teachers and parents…the ultimate authorities. I countered this negative training by "thinking." I woke up every morning at about 4 AM and lay still, thinking for two hours. If you "think" about it, one can think of a lot of stuff in two hours; then add on two hours every day and it became addictive. It did not bother me to be awake, actually, I treasured the quiet time. I thought about what had happened yesterday, what might happen today, was I prepared? Did I do my homework? Did I like whoever had interacted with me yesterday? What else could I have said or done? All of the: "I should have said's, and why didn't I remember this's?" I thought about religion and God and developed, for me, satisfactory answers to questions related to many subjects. I learned to question everything by taking "positions" and supporting or attacking them from many sides. The most important thing that I learned, which I still treasure today, was to trust my brain. For a nine year old this was a major and dangerous revelation.

As I was lying in bed on Saturday, doing my early morning "think," the Science Fair project idea came to me, and I got up and started working. I will build a SUBMARINE, I thought. It will need to work: float, submerge, suspend motionless in the water and then resurface. First I needed a plan, so I drew one…a rough outline of my version of a World War II submarine, scaled down to 18 inches long. I had made model airplanes and boats: some from scratch, some from kits, using balsa-wood. I used left over pieces to construct the submarine.

I started and soon realized the need for the ballast/water/submersion tank. I knew, from having watched movies about submarines, that they had water tanks that could be filled with water or pumped out, which changed their buoyancy from positive to negative, causing the submarine to submerge, surface, or to be suspended. Having no guidelines, I improvised. Mother gave me an empty, plastic shampoo bottle which held about 8 ounces. I drilled one small hole in it on each end—one hole in the top and one in the bottom. I told Dad what I was doing, and he supplied me with about 8 feet of transfusion tube, the kind used in hospitals for intravenous drips. I glued the tubing into the holes in the ends of the "submersion tank"…er shampoo bottle. The idea was to have one tube let water into or force it out of the tank, and the other tube on the other end of the tank could let air out or blow air into the tank, which I could control by sucking on or blowing into the tube…sucking slowly filled the bottle, and blowing forced the water out. Then I glued the bottle to the bottom of the sub, about in the middle of the boat. Finally the rest of the sub was built up with planking, bent around frames. Each plank was glued individually until the body of the sub was built up enough so that I could glue the deck on. I drilled one hole in the deck through which I ran the long tube which I held in my hand, at ready for the sucking or blowing. Then I attached a very short piece of hose to the bottom of the tank and ran it through the bottom of the sub. This was the water inlet and outlet to the tank, easily controlled by sucking or blowing. The sub could be suspended in water by crimping the transfusion tube, which held the water in the tank at a stationary level. Before gluing on the top deck, I filled up the sub with sand. This allowed me to shake the model back— forth and side to side to balance and adjust the weight perfectly (after several tries) so that the sub floated level on the surface. I finished the boat off with a conning tower, a gun, and a railing around the deck and on the conning tower which was made with a hundred staples glued end to end. Painted battleship grey, it looked great.

I had even angled the water tank/shampoo bottle so that when the transfusion tube was sucked on, the sub dived nose first, and when I blew into the tube to force the water out of the tank, the sub rose up bow first. We tested the sub in a big fish tank, and it worked perfectly.

BUT four days before the Science Fair, Dan, yes, my innocent younger brother, came up with a brilliant idea. Why not submerge the sub in our third floor bathtub, which was far away from our ever vigilant Mother, and try depth-charging it? Of course, this would be the true test. We would use one of our "two inchers." A two incher was a two inch long firecracker...really a small stick of dynamite. We knew that the wick on the two-incher burned internally and would not only burn under water but also ignite the dynamite. This should be a real test, because we knew the two-incher was powerful...an empty quart tin-can placed over the firecracker would blow up into the air well over 100 feet. We had done this several times with satis- fying results: it even brought out the police and prompted nasty calls from the spinster Baldwin sisters who lived next door and had been major participants in the "Murgatroid" and "Brushball" incidents.

The bathtub on the third floor was installed in 1900, and was a huge, deep, almost seven foot long, claw-footed masterpiece. Ideal for floating the candle powered "put-put boats," which we jazzed up by burning rubbing alcohol to increase the heat and speed, and although we had no battery powered, ready-to-run toys, we had wonderful and dangerous gasoline, alcohol, and candle-powered toys (which would, because of attorneys and safety concerns, never be allowed on the market after 1980.) And that old tub became our indoor, rainy-day haven.

Never having done this before, we had no inkling of what we were in for. First we filled the tub with about seventy-five gallons of water, bringing it to the safety overflow limit. Next we tied a rock to the "depth charge," lit the fuse and dropped it into the water. Spewing bubbles from the burning fuse, it settled to the bottom of the bathtub about a foot from the sub. We leaned over the tub, watching the depth charge as it sat next to the sub on the bottom of the tub. And, nothing happened. "Maybe it's a dud," said Dan. "Yup," I agreed intelligently rubbing my chin…KABOOM!! Most of the water in the tub, along with pieces of submarine and sand, erupted in a huge geyser, hitting the ceiling, splaying out to cover the walls and blowing both Dan and me up, back, and onto our rear ends, covering the floor with water, smashing the ceiling light and plunging us into semi-darkness!

It was a truly spectacular explosion, causing Mother, who was on the first floor in the kitchen to call out "Yoohoo, you boys get down here, right now!!" But we were deafened by the blast, even though it was under water, and truly didn't hear her clearly.

And we were trying to recover—in shock and speechless, wiping off pieces of submarine and covered with a sandy muck, celebrating over how totally successful the depth charge had been. Slapping each other on the back while trying to recover, we had a moment of pure, terrified joy! Then panic set in. "Jeeeeez, look at this room…a gawdaful mess!" said Dan

"I can't believe it. There's nothing left of the sub the…Here comes Mother!! Quick, close the door. Lock it. Shhsssss," I whispered, as if being quiet now could save us from discovery.

"Just what are you two doing in there?" Mother's non-questioning accusatory voice froze us in place as she arrived at the door.

"Uh, nothing, Mother. I think Dan has diarrhea…"

"Diarrhea? Nonsense. Now you both come right out of there! Is that water coming under the door?"

"Yes, Mother, unh, Dan overflowed the tub by accident taking a bath."

"I did not!" said Dan. "You blew up the sub!"

"Bobby, were you playing with firecrackers in the house? You open that door, right now!"

And so it came to pass that I was in trouble again, and I learned how to clean a bathroom from top to bottom and to let go of my totally destroyed physical world, and to put the mix of tragedy and success behind me...sort-of.

Big problem: I had blown up my Science Fair project, and when I told Doc Walters about the spectacular success of the depth-charge, he was not amused and informed me that I would make another submission ready for the Science Fair, "or else!" I had never before had an "or else" from Doc...I had endured several "or elses" from other adults and kids, but this one was serious. The worst thing about this was that I had let Doc down, and I felt so bad that I stayed up all night for two nights—literally working "day and night" and successfully built a second, even better model submarine that was ready just in time for the Fair. It won honorable mention in the Science Fair, Abram London took first prize for his experiment with penicillin. Abe's project was truly impressive. Penicillin was a the new "miracle drug" at that time

As was often the case, I did not even suspect what a great memory this would become.

PS. Later that Winter, the submarine mysteriously "disappeared" from its display spot on the small table in the front hall of our house: I searched the house thoroughly looking for it to no avail...I repeatedly unsuccessfully interrogated all family members, perhaps...it is in the attic.

PAM AND THE CARS

RS Wilkinson

The grease would not wash out. It was imbedded under my nails, into all of the cracks in the skin of my hands. I scrubbed with a stiff brush using GoJo, a powerful new hand cleaner used by automobile mechanics. I thought I was clean, I was told that at least it was "honest dirt," but most of the girls that I knew did not agree...I was not completely clean, which put a huge restriction on what I could and could not touch, which was very bad because girls were already mostly untouchable. In 1952 I accepted that "no" meant no. Most of us had been taught that from early childhood, and it was not considered arguable. So when Dad said "No" to my request of a loan to buy my first car, I did not even try persuasion. I clearly remembered the "no loan for Bobby" bicycle incident, so instead I got a job pumping gas, greasing cars, and changing tires at Bill Strang's Texaco Station in Kenmore Square, Boston.

I think the 'no loan' thing was a result of my Dad's experience with his father: in 1920 Dad wanted to be a doctor, but his father would not pay for medical school because he wanted Dad to be a lawyer...so my father worked in the coal miles of Pennsylvania and borrowed money (at 22% interest from his uncle!) to pay for his tuition while attending The University of Pennsylvania Medical School. It took years for Dad to pay back the debt. For some reason, never explained, my siblings could borrow money, but I could not. Perhaps it was Dad's way of making me independent…if so, it sure worked.

Therefore, I got my first real job—a summer job. A dirty, exhausting, physical, low paying, 50 cents an hour, no benefits job (true, not as bad as mining coal) in the tradition of the real meaning of a JOB…just over broke, better save every nickel!

But I enjoyed being independent and working hard and was liked and respected by the other guys and by our good boss, Bill Strang, who at first wondered if a famous Doctor's son would really get his hands dirty. I knew that Mother thought working in a gas station: pumping gas, changing oil, fixing flats, greasing and doing all of the dirty maintenance associated with cars, was below me. But she did not offer to loan me the money for a car. I learned to enjoy the work, the respect and the companionship of the other "grease monkeys" in the garage. And amazingly, I saved $150.00 in two months—enough to buy my first car, a 1948 Oldsmobile convertible. I could even buy gas to go on a date. Those were the days of the "gas wars." Competing gas stations on opposite sides of Commonwealth Avenue were constantly underselling each other by one or two cents: sometimes regular was priced 17 or 18 cents a gallon. This was especially important because my Olds managed 13 miles per gallon, was heavy, rode like a big boat, steered like a truck with no power steering, mushed around corners as if it were plowing through peanut butter, and was tired and worn out at 48,000 miles. All of the steering ball joints and universal joints on all cars needed greasing at least every thousand miles—even with proper maintenance the engines and suspension systems needed repair and replacement at 70,000 miles—and because they did not last, $150.00 was a fair price for a four year old car. But my Olds was a convertible! This was VERY important, because if I wanted a good looking girl, or any girl to ride with me, (which I truly did) there were only two good cars: convertibles or hot rods. Not only did the cars not last very long mechanically, but they also seemed to be built to attract rust.

As bad as this sounds and was, these cars were far superior to anything on the market today for one very important reason: SEX! You bet. Bench seats, front and back, superior headroom, great legroom, no seatbelts or restraints, small windows and windshields: in other words they were great cars! No matter that the brakes in cars and trucks were terrible—apt to lock up any wheel at any time, the handling was mushy, and it took skill and practice to maintain control at sixty miles per hour. Panic stops required rapid pumping of the brakes…it was common knowledge that a well-controlled high speed slide around a corner could lean the car dramatically over and drift a girl sitting on the passenger side right into your lap. Yes, our techniques for getting acquainted were totally different from today's high tech, arm's length, computer driven communications.

And so it was because I had a convertible that I dared to ask out for a date the most beautiful girl that I had ever seen.

"Would you like to go dancing with me at Norumbega?"

"Yes," she said, "Where is it?"

She had accepted. I was struck dumb.

"You've never been there?"

"No—but I 've heard about it."

Norumbega Park, located in Newton, Mass. was a high-class place with tables, a dance floor, a twelve piece dance band…the works. It would cost about $8.00 per couple (two day's pay) to get a table, dance for two hours and drink a pitcher of fruit punch. You could also walk in the park which led to the Charles River, there were boat ramps and rental canoes. The canoes were 50 cents per hour.

"It's in Newton. It's nice. I think you'll like it." I tried to nod reassuringly. "I'll pick you up Saturday at 7:30, Is that OK?"

"Yes." She raised her eyebrows and looked directly at me.

I took a step back and asked: "Where do you live?" Wow, this was an impressive question—good one Bob—it showed that my brain was fried. The girl was sitting on the beach at Province Lake in New Hampshire. Nervously I realized I didn't know where she lived, and brilliantly concluded that this might be crucial information…so I smoothly added, "And what is your name?" Another good one I glumly thought. I did know her name, but had never before spoken to her. I was surprised when this awkward questioning actually worked.

"Pamela, call me Pam. I'll write my address if you can find me a pencil and paper."

The ball point pen had not yet been invented, so I ran back to my car, making sure she was watching me, pulled the lever to activate the mechanism that took down the top. This started a loud grinding noise, and slowly the top rose up like a giant wing, extending skyward, and then even more slowly folding into three sections and tucking down behind the rear seat. I exhaled in relief, because about 50% of the time the top would get stuck half-way up or down. This action was to subtly allow Pam to notice that I had a working convertible. Oh yeah, a really smooth move, Bob, I stupidly thought. Then I ran back to Pam and sat next to her on the beach.

My heart was pounding. I was literally terrified. Mother would not approve. Dad would not approve. They wanted me to date only girls with the proper background: which would be, of course, a doctor's daughter—Dad was a famous Doctor at the Lahey Clinic whose patients included Ty Cobb, Ted Williams, Yogi Berra, JFK, and The Baron Rothschild, who sent us wine every Christmastime. JFK was a Senator at this time. Mother had met him and said he was: "charming, intelligent, and might really become something!" The Clinic was then located at 605 Commonwealth Avenue in Boston, which also happened to be next to Bill Strang's Texaco station, and I had met all of these people because patients and doctors usually parked at Strang's parking lot. All I knew about Pam's "background" was that her father worked in the GE plant in Lynn, Mass. Certainly not nearly good enough for Mother. Then I thought about myself: a grease monkey—was I really any better? Mother had selected several girls for me to date, and I am sure they grew up to be beauties, and they did have the "proper background", but they struck me as exceedingly plain. Pam was a knockout! But Mother had repeatedly reminded us of the extreme importance of "proper background".

In 1938 Dad had bought an old farmhouse, complete with barn, on Province Mountain. It was a steal at $4,000, and we used it as a summer retreat for many years. It was, and still is, the only house on the north side of the mountain with a stunning view of the White Mountains. At the foot of the mountain, in Butler Field, there were about twenty campsites (there are many more now.) The camps were permanent; many were very comfortable well-equipped cabins. Most of the campers worked at the GE plant in Lynn, Mass. Many of them took their vacation during the first two weeks of July, and there were lots of kids my age to befriend. Almost daily during the summer I would go down to the beach to play with them or invite them to walk up the mile long road to our house. We would play games for hours—unsupervised: Hide and seek, kick the can, kickball, and mountain croquet…strange but true we had a croquet set in the field, complete with hills, lumps of turf, even pine cones as obstacles. It was great fun…the precious years when we were just friends. But Pam was dating a boy who was two years older than I, and they had never been up to play with us.

"I will need something to write on, and where is the pencil?" Pam looked up at me without moving her head—just eyes—and smiled the same knowing smile that Mother had used on me hundreds of times.

Oh my God, I thought. Don't tell me all women are alike!

Except—Pam's smile spread a warm ache over my whole stomach.

I shakily recovered from having completely forgotten my mission, and said: "I really don't need a pencil. Just tell me your address and I'll remember it."

"Really?"

"Really."

These incredibly impressive skills at the art of memory and conversation rewarded me with another smile.

"OK, I live at 34 Oak St. in Lynn—see you at 7:30. I'll be ready."

"Great," I said, standing and turning and running back to the car, feeling awkward and clumsy, and silently repeating the address several times, and then praying that the old flathead straight eight engine would start. It did. I exhaled in speechless relief again. Beautiful women still do this to me…I become monosyllabic.

What, in my self-centeredness I did not fully understand, was that a date with "The Doctor's" son could literally be a dream come true for Pam. I was the potential heir to "The Place on the mountain."

On Saturday I dressed in my best suit, which was my only suit. Pam was gorgeous...in a long white dress that was full rather than tight. We drove with the top down, and her hair blew softly up and side to side. Norumbega Park was full of kids that I knew. They did not serve any alcohol. This was before we even knew the word marijuana. We were all straight kids, very innocent. Almost all of us were virgins aged 16 to 18. We were very interested in sex. We just didn't know how to get it. Girls were very cautious because getting pregnant was the worst 'punishment' for having pre-marital sex. The concept of it being acceptable for a girl to be a single mother did not exist: most girls unfortunate enough to be "with child" either had shot gun weddings, or quietly put the baby up for adoption. Their reputations were ruined...it was considered a disgrace. Abortions were rare and never talked about. Boys accepted this too, and of course there was always the presence of the unfair 'double standard.' And most of us were too shy and young looking to attempt buying contraceptives, which one had to ask for from a druggist who was invariably standing behind a counter and gave disapproving looks while walking back to wherever contraceptives were kept. But I was so shy and unsure that none of these were my concerns. I just wanted her to like me.

As we entered the Norumbega dance hall and found an unoccupied table, everyone turned to stare. Pam was overwhelmingly attractive. Several of my friends: most of whom exuded a snobby superior attitude, and all of whom were children of doctors, lawyers or successful businessmen, sidled over to quietly ask me where I found her, where did she live, were we going steady, was she available?

This had never happened to me—it must be a dream. She had a wonderful soft, full voice. Her carriage, the way she walked and held herself, dominated the room. She was smooth on the dance floor, easily led, terrific at the waltz. I could feel the muscles in her back gently tighten and relax as we floated...yes, a dream. She had no makeup on...only a subtle lipstick. Her skin glowed softly, was flawlessly smooth...reminded me of cool vanilla ice cream. As we danced I looked at our intertwined hands. She did not seem to mind my almost-clean, calloused, work hands. I wanted to kiss her, to taste her. She smelled like a spring bouquet. I held her, dancing for an hour. Then, because I wanted to hug her and was having trouble refraining, I suggested we walk to the river, which we did. Pam spotted the canoes lined up upside-down on the dock.

"Do you know how to canoe?" She looked at me with eyes that said, "I hope so."

"Oh yes, I've been in many canoes…let's rent one."

"Oh good," she said, "You can show me how."

I found the attendant and gave him 50 cents. "Be back in an hour," he reminded.

The attendant, a boy about my age, could not take his eyes off of Pam. He held the canoe as I showed Pam how to step into the middle, leaning over to hold the gunwales to steady the canoe while sitting slowly down onto the small seat. She followed my example perfectly, gracefully, and we were off. I paddled slowly up-stream knowing that I could drift back. It was calm, quiet, about 80 degrees, and we were alone on the historic Charles River.

After paddling for about twenty minutes, I put the paddle down and let the canoe drift. I could not think of anything intelligent to say, so we were quiet. It was beautiful. Pam had taken her shoes off at my suggestion when she entered the canoe. They were beautiful silver slippers. I picked one of them up holding it above her. It was almost dark. Even my hands looked clean and soft…and quietly I told her she was Cinderella, and I would like to be her prince.

I whispered, "Hold your foot up, and I will see if the shoe fits."

She smiled softly and breathed, "Yes."

I slowly leaned over her and she turned, raising her arms to meet me, and Whoosh, with hardly a splash, we turned over. The river was shallow, we were near the shore, and we floundered our way back to the dock, dragging the canoe with us. Emerging from the river we were a sight to behold, or at least the attendant thought so because he was laughing so hard he could not help us out.

We returned the canoe and brushed off bits of river grass and mud, but it was hopeless. The only exit was back through the ballroom/dining area, and I had to pay the bill. We tried to walk through this gauntlet with dignity, but every step I took made a loud squishing noise because my shoes were full of water, and Pam had lost one of her slippers, so my Cinderella was limping and squishing alternately. The ignominy was complete, augmented by the uncontrollable waves of laughter, giggles and pointing that had replaced the jealous glares of the other girls as they gleefully watched us drip and squish dejectedly out the door.

Pam would not look at me. I did not put down the convertible top. We rode in silence. She never said a word—all the way to Lynn—about a thirty-five minute drive. I did not know what to do or say…It was irreparable. Pam never, ever spoke to me again. I felt that I had destroyed the promise of life, of love, of happiness for both of us…I was inexcusably guilty.

I did go back the next day to Norumbega—to the boat dock and the river and waded through the muck until I found her silver slipper. I cleaned it up with GoJo and mailed it to her address with a short note: Pam, I Love you. I should have tried again—taken the slipper to her, asked for forgiveness, for one more date…it has left me with an empty place in my heart.

I hope after all of these years her memory of this evening, like mine, is of the magic and not the mud.

THE SPECTATOR

RS Wilkinson

In the fall of 1952, I was a senior at B&N, a private day school in Cambridge. But this story really starts when I was in the fourth grade in the John D. Runkle School in Brookline, Mass. I was given an IQ test. That's right. Dr. Watson, a fleshy man dressed in a three piece, pin striped suit complete with a bow tie, addressed us as "little children". He had a very squeeky, high, pitched voice. We instantly disliked him…intensely. We were NOT little children; we were fourth graders!

Dr. Watson introduced himself and proclaimed that he would administer a new (IQ tests were very new) test that would tell us how smart we really were. Brookline had a reputation for "Smart" kids. There were 34 of us in the classroom, and 30 were Jewish. None of us really knew what the difference between the Christian and Jewish faiths were, but we all knew that on Jewish Holidays there was almost nobody in school, which was great for kids because we were either out of school or had no work to do. Plus when you combined the religious holidays with the regular holidays, we had an impressive number of no-schoolwork days.

Being in a predominantly Jewish school was very difficult on us of other faiths because the Jewish kids were smart. Not just a little smart…WAY smart. And they did their homework, which was even worse! The parents were partially to blame because when I left for school, my Mother would ask if I had my lunch with me, but Bobby Stein's parents would ask: "Did you finish all of your homework, and do you have all of your books with you?" It was almost impossible to compete with that.

We did not know what an IQ test was, but I feared the worst… my stupidity would be exposed again. Sure enough, Dr. Watson explained the new, multiple choice, fill-in-the-blank-with-a-special-pencil-test. I remember thinking: "Oh boy, never had this kind of test, and I don't like this Watson guy." But I took the test as instructed, except for one thing: I had somehow aligned the questions and answers incorrectly and had jumped over a column of answers. This meant that when I got to the last page of questions, I had no match-ing answer column. Not wishing to expose my stupidity and lack of attention to following instructions, I simply searched for and found the empty answer column and filled it in.

The following week the Principal called my parents in to a meeting in his office and announced that I had scored so low in IQ that I could not even tie my shoes! He further explained that I must be cheating in class in order to have passed any courses and recommended that I withdraw from school to be tutored. They had discovered that I was even stupider than I thought I was. This would have been a bad situation for any kid, but it was even worse for me, a genius who thought, along with everybody else, that he was an idiot. (Please understand that all of the watered-down euphemisms now used to describe my situation did not even exist then.) Fortunately my parents knew that I was not THAT stupid, and they immediately enrolled me in another school—the Park School, which was over two miles from our house.

I mention this because, weather permitting, I walked to and from school. I am sure the walk was good for me…it allowed me to spend more time thinking, and I had a lot to think about. I had to make new friends, adjust to new teachers, and decide what to do about bullies. The bullies I noticed were usually boys, and they were often teasing girls…pulling their hair, especially if they had braided hair, taunting them with words and making fun of their lesser physical abilities: especially if the girl(s) were smarter which they invariably were, or so it seemed to me. And one day a big kid, George McDundle, grabbed one of the girls, Mabel, whom I liked because she talked to me about important stuff: like how to do the math homework. George spun her around by her hair, causing her to cry in pain. This I could not tolerate, and because I was considerably smaller than George, I ran up to him, and without warning, punched him as hard as I could in the nose. Stunned, he sat down suddenly and grabbed his bloody nose. Then he stood up and aimed a punch at me, but he missed so I punched him in the mouth. Then I said: "Don't ever tease girls again or I'll really get you!" As with most of our "fights" two punches ended it. George started crying, and I was immediately collared and jerked back by our Phys-Ed teacher who was supposed to be maintaining order at recess.

We were all marched into the principal's office, and fortunately this time I had a credible witness, the Phys-ED teacher, and he had seen the entire event. Hence, I was reprimanded in private by the Principal and told: "I do not approve of fighting, but George deserved what you did to him; just don't ever tell anyone I said that to you. Now promise me that." I promised never to say a word about it. " Now, I'll call your parents, and you go straight home—you're suspended for the rest of the day." And so I walked the two miles, slowly, back to not being able to tell my parents what had happened at school. And I thought: Man, being a kid is tough—you can't tell the truth about what happened even when you have a credible witness!

George never teased the girls again, at least not that I saw, and I survived the fifth grade and returned in the sixth grade to the Runkle School. I was not happy there, partly because the IQ test had left the teachers with a lasting impression of my dumbness which I was not smart enough to overcome. But then came the "water bomb" incident. I did have two teachers I liked—which was a record for me— Miss Daily and Mr. Wintermeyer. Miss Daily I liked by accident: one day at the end of lunch period, I was running through the hall and around a corner, running fast in order not to be late for class, when suddenly in front of me was Miss Daily. Too late—I couldn't stop, so I put up my hands to soften the collision and SQUISH both of my hands met her soft, beautiful breasts. I did not knock her down, but the expression of astonishment on both of our faces told of my innocence and of her annoyance. While I was apologizing she was saying: "Don't you ever do that again!!" And so I promised never to run in the hallways, and it was a long time before I could look her in the eyes.

John Lewis, another of my best friends who was called Whiff or Whiffle because of his super-short haircut, taught me how to fold a single piece of composition paper so that it made a hollow paper ball about the size of a baseball. The paper ball could be filled with water at a drinking fountain, and it would hold water for about 30 seconds before starting to leak. My classroom was on the third floor, and the stairs wound around the stairwell so that I could lean over the banister and see all the way down to the first floor. Yes, I thought, I can drop the water-bomb down three floors and it will make a sensational splash. The next time I had Miss Daily in class, I asked to be "excused" to go to the "bathroom," a name that confused me because we never took a bath there, stopped at the water fountain, filled my already prepared water-bomb, leaned over the banister and dropped it, watching it fall three stories and splatter on the floor just at the feet of the principal. Instantly my moment of excitement over a job well done turned into terror. I raced back to class and sat down, head down, concentrating on schoolwork. Not two minutes behind me, the principal entered the room—his shoes, socks and pants were splattered with water, and when he asked Miss Daily if any students had asked to be excused during the last five minutes. I knew I was a goner. Trying not to gulp, I felt like a fish out of water gasping for air. Miss Daily looked around the room, looked at the principal, made eye contact with me for a nanosecond, and then slowly shook her head...no. The principal spun around and left, heading for the next classroom. I was truly astounded. It was the first, and as I can attest at 80 years old, the rare time that a person put her or him-self at risk to cover for me...guilty or not. I don't know why she did this, but it totally changed my behavior. I quit the bad boy act...well most of it, and as with many "reformed" people, I became intolerant of "bad" acts of mischief done by others.

In the seventh grade I had Mr. Wintermeyer for science. He was my first male teacher, and I liked him and the way he taught science, and I earned my first "A" in school in his class. He had been a fighter pilot in WWII, and described in class some of his heroic, near-death experiences…often including questions challenging us to answer: "what would you do next?" He told my parents I was "head and shoulders" above the rest of the class in problem solving. It was my first compliment from a teacher, so I guess you could say that he and Miss Daily had a lasting positive effect on me. It did not make me a good boy. I managed a severe reprimand for fighting for the infamous "drinking-fountain water incident." It was another bully scene: A big eighth grader, a boy known for picking on smaller boys and girls: shoving them, bumping into them, knocking them onto the ground when they weren't looking, especially at the drinking-fountai, Mac, as he was called, liked pushing kids out of his way and barging to the front of the line at the drinking fountain as recess was ending. We would all line up for a quick drink of water, and one day Mac pushed a small girl out of the way, knocking her down so that she "scun-up" her knees and hands on the ground. I was next in line, and once again I became the "avenger." As Mac leaned over the drinking fountain, I pushed down hard on his head, forcing his mouth into the metal shoe-horn-like guard that covered the spout hole. And as he straightened his back and stood up, I punched him in the nose. This was, by the way, the most often punched place in the playground "disputes" which occurred almost daily.

Which brings up, also by the way, the huge difference between life as a boy in 1947 as compared to now, 2015. You know that we had no computers, cell phones, digital cameras, and almost no parental or even adult supervision over our playgrounds. After school in the grade school, grades one through eight, most of us would go to the Dean Rd. playground and "play" without protective gear. We had no head, elbow or knee guards, and even playing tackle football (it was always tackle) only a few of us had helmets, and they were of the old leather construction with no face protection at all…sort of like Snoopy's Red Baron. This led to numerous cuts scrapes and bruises, all of which were healed by applying ice and Band-Aids…I do not recall even one trip to a hospital. We chose up teams for our improvised versions of football, baseball, kickball, kick the can, dodgeball, and in the winter sledding and skating. The skating was done on flooded tennis courts, which in the summer were free for use by all. Very few of us had tennis rackets, so the courts were never crowded. Our only adult supervision was Tommy, a foot patrolman we all knew and loved. We never called him a Cop. Tommy settled arguments and stopped the rare fistfight. Even more interesting, Tommy only walked through the playground three or four times per afternoon while making his "rounds." We had no fear of perverts or abduction—there were no such problems. I know, we were not in the inner city, but the playground was less than two hundred feet from Beacon St. right on the edge of Boston. WWII had ended in 1945, so that worry, complete with air raid drills, had ended. We were truly free to be kids—just kids—our only outside influence was the radio: "The Lone Ranger," "The Shadow," "Mr. and Mrs. North." And if you could handle it: "Innersanctum," a scary precursor to the Alfred Hitchcock brand of suspense. These were all radio shows to which we needed special permission to listen. Some of them were broadcast on Fridays, even as late as 9PM—way beyond our bedtime.

Yes, we had rules and regulations, and manners…most of which seem to be long gone. What were they? Most bedtimes up through the eighth grade, were eight O'clock during week nights…maybe as late as 9:30 or 10:00 on weekends. Bedtime meant we were in bed, quiet, lights out, and radios if we had one which was rare, were turned off. In most homes, everybody was required to make it to breakfast, and to be up early enough to help with breakfast chores: setting the table, cleaning up, etc. There was no sleeping late except on Saturdays. We had to be home by 5:30 every night for dinner, and that meant washed up and changed into clean clothes and ready to help with setting the table, clearing the table and doing the dishes— every day. We did not complain or whine—it was not tolerated . We were required to help with all "chores": cleaning, taking out the trash, yard-work, cleaning up our rooms…all easy stuff, really, in return for the afternoon playtime freedom. Try to imagine more than a hundred kids playing together for two to three hours, Monday through

Friday, with no adult supervision and no fear. We were earning the priceless freedom to just be kids. Claire, my wife, grew up on a farm in Salisbury, Mass. She also had similar chores with additional "farm oriented" responsibilities and hours of playtime freedom.

And we did have manners: Look people in the eye and shake hands and repeat their names when saying hello; stand up and step aside to offer your chair or seat on the couch or in a train or trolley or streetcar to any older person who entered a room or vehicle (this meant any time;) answers were "yes sir," or " yes mam"; hold the door for women entering or leaving a building or automobile; always offer to carry any package that an older person or woman was carrying. At the table the adults were served first and no one ate a thing until the oldest person had picked up a utensil and started eating. If you think this is too much to ask…just imagine it now, and imagine how truly NICE it would be to have this sense of peace and order and respect…

We were not disrespectful to adults or authority figures, and did not yell, swear, use foul language or fight in the presence of adults, and most of the time, the adults were similarly restrained in our presence, and if they slipped up, they would apologize for it!

And so, after I punched out Mac at the drinking fountain, I expected to be in big trouble again, but Miss Daily had seen the event, and once again I had a credible witness, and she spoke up in my defense, and I was saved. Another lesson learned: that women will often speak up against injustices that men will tolerate as "just part of life."

BUT this is not really what this story is about, because after graduating the eighth grade I had to enroll in the ninth grade, and it had to be in a different school, high school.

Because my record was so bad academically and behaviorally, Mom and Dad decided my only hope was to go to a private school, and they submitted an application for me to a school in Cambridge, Mass. called "Browne and Nichols"…B&N. I was not acceptable based on my past record, but fortunately the Director of Admissions, who was a man, actually delegated the work to a really wonderful woman named Muriel Page, who was also the school secretary, and who, like many secretaries actually ran everything. She asked me the most terrifying question: "Have you ever had an IQ test?"

Well, since I never really answered the test correctly, and since they never actually gave me a score, and since I did not even know what a "good" score was…I sort of fibbed and said: "No."

Miss Page looked kindly at me, smiled and said: "Well, let's just sit down and take one now. This won't hurt, and I am sure you will do well."

The truth is that this was the second time I recall an adult telling me I could do well at anything…a moment I am sure many of us remember clearly. I sat, and she administered the test, and because she said: "This is a timed test, but relax and just do as well as you can," and she smiled at me, I relaxed. The test was interesting this time, I actually enjoyed it…what a difference a good person makes… she took a few minutes and looked over the test. Then she said: "The school psychologist (I thought oh no, another Dr. Watson!) will grade this, but I can tell you that you did very well…actually better than any other student I've seen." I waited for the "but"…instead she said that the school would be in touch with my parents. That was that. The "school" called the next day and said that I had been accepted. I was excited and scared. The good news was that apparently I was not an idiot.

My ninth grade English teacher was Gilbert Graves, whom everyone called "Gibby." He was a big man, with striking, blue eyes and a wonderful, warm, ringing, deep voice that resonated with kindness and enthusiasm and authority, and he was the school's Wrestling coach. So, after playing football in the fall, I signed up for Wrestling as my winter sport, and it changed my life. The exposure in Wrestling is very intimidating…terrifying at first: you wear almost no clothes, you are alone on the mat, everyone is looking at you, and there is no one else to blame for failure. If your self-confidence is low, as was mine and almost all beginning "wrestlers," it takes a total and concentrated mental effort just to get out on the mat. Even worse, it is the most exhausting eight minutes that I have ever experienced. However, when you win the match, the success is all yours.

In the 1950's, the matches lasted eight minutes and were divided into three periods: two minutes where each boy started standing up, then three minutes where one boy would start in the top position and, finally, after a one minute break, three minutes where the other boy would start in the top position. The scoring was precise and complex, with points awarded for performing certain moves or gaining positional holds, and a "Pin" ended the match. A pin was awarded when one boy held the other boy's shoulder blades pressed to the mat for three seconds. At the match's conclusion, if there was not a "pin"...whoever had the most points was declared the winner. We always shook hands, and the referee would signify the winner by grasping his wrist and raising it high over his head. In the 1960's the matches were reduced to six minutes with three two-minute periods.

When I started wrestling in the ninth grade I was physically weak, nervous and clueless. My older brother, Dave, who was a superior athlete, had preceded me...earning an exceptional record as a wrestler at B&N. This was bad for me in two ways: the opposition thought because we were brothers that I would be tough competition, and that Dave must have taught me, so I must know something about wrestling. Well, Dave was four years older, and he had avoided me "like the plague" because he considered me his nosey, tattletale, "out-of-it" little brother. What Dave did give me was a sense of humor, fairness and honesty...well most of the time. We had already learned that the world was dominated by liars and that telling the truth was extremely dangerous—possibly fatal...that the truth often caused much more damage than a lie, and that truth-tellers were much more vigorously discredited and punished than liars. This fact was established early in my life and re-established many times. This may sound negative or cynical, but I was never negative. I had learned to trust my mind, and with wrestling I learned it was a mind game of split second reflexes and decisions, and that the true danger came from the novice and/or slow-thinking wrestler that didn't know what he was doing.

Because my muscles had not yet developed, I was known as a skill wrestler, but this took three painful years of learning the hard way—by losing. Most important: something new developed, and this was experience supported self-confidence which partly, because wrestling was such an "exposure" sport, translated into a confidence in other "exposure" ventures, such as: coaching wrestling, teaching, being the boss, starting businesses, starting schools, boat building, house building, sailing, being fired—twice...and generally having fun and causing a lot of trouble along the way.

My next boost in confidence came in Hal Melcher's English class. I was transferred from James Ducey's eleventh grade "B" section up to Melcher's "A" section after I impressed them with my interpretation of Whitman's poem: "To a Skylark". As a new student in Melcher's English class, I wrote a story called, "Nearly Through." It described an aging prizefighter, needing money, fighting a much younger boxer...a sort of last stand to pay some bills in a losing, take-a-beating fight. A sad story. When I finished reading it, the class was silent. Then Mr. Melcher said: "That was excellent. We'll put it in the "Spectator", which was the school's quarterly magazine, of which he was the faculty advisor. With his encouragement, I wrote many other stories and became, in my senior year, Editor of the "Spectator". One of my many significant contributions to B&N resulted from this position of authority. Indeed it was authority: I was responsible for all of the editing, much of the writing, the layout, the printing, all of the typing (remember the day of proofs, then galley proofs, pasted layouts—all replaced by the digital/electronic world?) And, as Editor in Chief I wrote the Editorial.

B&N had just, in 1952, completed building a new gymnasium, with an ice hockey rink and basketball court and a wrestling room. I suggested to all of the authorities in order: Dave, the Head of Maintenance, Bill, the Director of Athletics, and finally Mr. Pratt, the Headmaster, that it would be beneficial to all if the new Gymnasium could be open to student use on Saturdays. I had thought of several reasons to bolster my pitch: it would keep us off the streets of Cambridge and Boston; the extra practice would make our teams better, it would be good for our health and school spirit, and it might even encourage alumni to contribute more to our athletic program. Unfortunately I was met by the proverbial stone wall...NO. Nobody wanted to donate the extra time, and I couldn't convince Mr. Pratt to pay for the extra supervision, SO…I used my editorial power and dedicated the early winter issue of the "Spectator" to the cause. I thought I did a good job. The cover featured two pictures: one showing the gym full of kids playing basketball, with the single question under the picture: "This?"-the other showing the Basketball court empty, with the question: "Or This?"

The editorial I wrote appeared on the next page, explaining the whole situation as I saw it, including my reasons for opening the gym on Saturdays and the objections that had been presented to me against the opening.

The "Spectator" was distributed on a Friday. I thought it looked great, but I was a little concerned that everything was quiet on the weekend…not one telephone call. On Monday I was just walking into school, and the first person I met at the door was my French teacher, Mr.Kenny. He smiled, then sadly and knowingly shook his head and softly whispered words that I shall and should never forget: "Stick your little neck out…chop, chop." Well I knew he knew French, but I didn't know he knew about life. The thing about "chop, chop" was that it represented a complete disconnect…I mean, like Bulkington in the "Lee Shore" chapter of <u>Moby Dick</u>. Once you leave conventional thinking, you can never go back. If you try to "go back," you will never be trusted or accepted. I was figuratively beheaded. Mr. Kenny added: "And Mr. Pratt would like to see you in his office."

The office had several semi comfortable chairs set in a semi-circle around his massive desk. I had been there before…also in his office was the faculty advisor to the "Spectator," Mr. Melcher, who was also my English teacher and a football coach. I was a "three-letter" athlete for the school: varsity football, wrestling and baseball. In football I was a quarterback (second string) on offense, and a linebacker on defense. I was the best tackler on the team and led the defense. I was definitely on the defense here, and my mind flashed back to an experience I had with Mr. Melcher six weeks ago: Melcher said, "Wilkinson, you are not taking the proper stance on defense… get ready as if you are about to defend a run." I knew he wanted me in a "three point stance"—bending over forward with feet spread and both knuckles on the ground. Instead I took an almost standing stance. I did this for two reasons: because I was only 5'9" tall, and it gave me better vision of the offensive players, and it allowed a quicker reaction to lateral movement. Melcher looked at me with disgust and suddenly launched himself full speed into me, his arms pushing me over backwards until I fell flat on my back. He continued his forward motion, landing on top of me and pushing my head and neck into the ground. It hurt physically and mentally. I was astounded by both his actions and the obvious dislike of me that showed on his face. When I could, I asked why he did this without any warning, and he replied: "Always be prepared for the unexpected."

I again saw on Melcher's face the same look of disgust and distaste, but this time his veins—neck veins and forehead veins, were swollen and flushed. Pratt had evidently just verbally knocked Melcher on his back, blaming him for allowing the publication of the "Spectator" with "those awful pictures and horrible editorial." Melcher was supposed to oversee, read, edit and censor the entire publication, but he had succumbed to Joseph Conrad's "flabby devil" and left the entire job to me. He was so angry he was speechless. Pratt looked at me and asked: "And, young man, just what have YOU learned from this?"

I knew exactly what I should say, but the hours of "thinking" as well as the composure under pressure that my wrestling experience gave me, combined with my bully-vengeance experiences, led me to quietly say: "Always be prepared for the unexpected."

Melcher started to his feet, but Pratt raised his voice, saying: "Wilkie, you will not publish another word unless it is read and cleared by Mr. Melcher...understood?" Ed Pratt always called me Wilkie, and the nickname stuck for years.

"Yes, sir."

"And, if you were not in your senior year, there would be much sterner punishment for your insubordinate and selfish actions...you have no idea how much reaction your little stunt caused with The Board of Trustees! You have managed to make many people very unhappy with you. Now, stay out of trouble for the rest of this year... this may have to go on your college report. You are dismissed."

I left the room not knowing if he meant that I was dismissed from school too. Suddenly nobody wanted to be seen talking with me…no students, no faculty. I received many whispered, "I told you so's." But actually no students had warned me about an adverse reaction to the "open the gym on Saturday plan" because they were all in favor of it. And yes, it came to pass at the school assembly three days later: Mr. Pratt announced that he had decided to proceed with a plan to open the gym, on a limited basis, of course, to students in good standing, for a limited number of hours, yet to be determined, on Saturdays.

So, who says you can't change the world? I had learned that William Faulkner was mostly right—if you want to change something—to make it better, or to right a wrong or an injustice, you need the very young or the very old to act. Everybody else is covering his or her reputation, job, position, or possible promotion: victims of the Flabby Devil. I had decided because of this incident, that it was worth the risk, whatever that might be, in return for knowing that I had tried. After all, I was one of the "very young."

And the Gym is still open on Saturdays.

And if Hal Melcher hadn't taught me to write…and to read and understand Faulkner, or if Gibby Graves hadn't taught me to prepare, and encouraged me to stand, never quit and take the heat,

or if I hadn't gone on to Middlebury College where I met and studied under the poet, John Berryman while studying for my MA degree…then you would not get to read about how I made another great contribution to B&N…of which I am also proud. Described in the chapter: "The Troublemaker."

MY FIRST DAY TEACHING

RS Wilkinson

January 11, 1961 and the first question I fielded as a teacher was: "Are you the new teach?"

I was not prepared for this scene. I had graduated Middlebury College as an English major two days ago and was starting a forty-five year careening career in teaching. My grade school experience of "orderly" classes was a far reach from this scene. Mr. Blander, the Principal at the Lyman C. Hunt School met with me at 7:45 AM and prepared me by saying: "This class, eighth grade, has been a problem…it has behaved so badly that my first teacher this year lasted only a month. The second teacher, a woman, an ex-military person, a sergeant, lasted six weeks, and now we cannot get any substitute teacher to even take the class for a day." Blander shook his head sadly and continued: "The sergeant did have some control, but I had to let her go because she slapped one of the boys in the face so hard that I was afraid his parents would sue us. And she said she would do it again if the little brats disrespected her—I had to let her go." He shook his head again, sadly. "She was the only teacher that even had a modicum of control with this class. The girls are as bad as the boys. Many of them, especially the boys, are almost 16 years old—just waiting to drop out of school. Do you think you can handle them?"

"I'll give it a try," I said, then added "I can do this—I like kids."

Blander gave me a long, slow skeptical look, then said: "OK, the bell rings at 8 o'clock, you will have five minutes to take attendance, get the hot lunch count, and collect five cents from students who want extra milk. There are thirty-six students in your eighth grade homeroom and you will be teaching them English, and you will also have two other English classes and a class in Science and one in Math. It is a six period day. You will have one free period, and you will have Cafeteria duty, which means you eat lunch there too…any questions?"

"Ah…seating charts, lesson plans, teacher's texts??"

"They are probably in the teacher's desk in the front of the room. Good Luck."

And thus, totally improperly prepared, I walked down the hall to my classroom and entered it at exactly 8:00 AM.

There were over thirty children—some were sitting on desks, some were on the floor, a boy and a girl were on the floor in the back of the room pretending to "make out," spitballs and crunched-up paper snowballs were being flung around the room. It was bedlam. I looked on the desk—no seating chart. Quickly I opened the desk drawers—no seating chart, no lesson plans, no teacher's texts… nothing.

I went to the blackboard and found a small piece of chalk and in big letters printed my name: MR. WILKINSON.

The class suddenly went quiet, and the big boy, the class bully I later learned, who had been lying on the floor with the girl, slowly stood up and asked, "Are you the new teach?"

"Yes," I replied very softly. "My name is Mr. Wilkinson." And I pointed to my name on the blackboard.

"You won't last two weeks," sneered the boy who was two inches taller than I, smirking and nodding cockily.

Slowly I walked to the back of the room, stepping over two kids on the floor, reached out and grabbed the boy by his shoulders—at the base of his neck—squeezed hard and pushed him back against the blackboard in the back of the room, looked into his eyes and very quietly and slowly said: "If you ever say anything like that to me again, you will not last two minutes."

Although I was only five feet ten inches tall I was very strong, and I squeezed hard on the muscles that connect the neck and shoulders.

The room was totally quiet. I could hear people breath. I waited a few seconds then asked, "What is your name?"

"RRRonald," came the shaky reply. I still held Ronald in my shoulder grip, and tears started down his cheeks. Then I turned Ronald around, put my left arm around his shoulders and walked him slowly to the front of the room, very quietly saying: "Ronald, you're my man. I am putting you in charge of taking attendance, writing down the hot lunch count and collecting a nickel from those who want extra milk with lunch." I finished with a barely audible: "Everybody get into your assigned seat." I stood with my arm around Ronald for a few seconds, spotted a girl sitting in the front row and said: "Please give Ronald some paper and something to write with." She did. Everybody sat in seats and Ronald took attendance in total quiet. He collected the nickels for milk and turned to me.

"Good job, Ronald," I said. "Now please take the money and attendance to the school office, and leave the door to the class-room open."

Then I pulled a sheet of paper out of my own briefcase, placed it on the end desk in the front row and said, " Please pass this along and clearly write or print your full name."

Then I signaled to the girl who had been lying on the floor with Ronald, beckoning her with my hand to come forward, and whispered to her: "Please go to the blackboard and draw a big check-erboard, draw six lines across and six lines down so that you have thirty six big squares...can you do this?" She frowned, so I repeated the whispered instructions, and then she nodded, walked along the board and drew lines that fairly neatly divided the whole board into squares.

"Very good," I said, "What is your name, please?"

"Victoria," she almost whispered.

"Pretty name. Now pretend that the squares represent the class-room, and draw one more at the top of the blackboard and write DESK in it." It took a couple of minutes for Victoria to figure out where to put my desk, but she did it. "Good job,' I said, "Now print your name in the square where you sit."

She did this. Now I at least knew two names I could put faces with. Then I asked the students, one by one, to go to the board and write their own name in the seating plan. The room was very quiet, and we were about half-finished with the names when the Principal peeked around the hall door and tiptoed into the classroom with Ronald in tow. He released Ronald and signaled for me to speak with him in the hall, so I softly told the class to continue writing their names on the blackboard –which they did.

The Principal whispered, "What did you do? Ronald has never been sent to the office except for swearing, fighting or disrespectful disobedience. And this classroom has always been so noisy that the hall door must be kept closed…did you hit someone?"

"No, but I did kind-of strangle Ronald for a minute."

Blander's eyes opened wide—"You strangled!..Is he OK?… We'll be sued!"

"He's fine," I said, "He's my man."

Blander looked at me, slowly shook his head twice, then turned to leave the room, "Be sure to talk with me before you leave this afternoon—if you make it that far." And he left, standing just out of sight to listen in the hallway.

The kids (I had a hard time calling them students) were finished writing their names on the board, and I asked the class who had the best handwriting?—big mistake I sensed, so I quickly rephrased the question: "I need a volunteer to copy down the seating chart on a piece of paper."

After a moment's hesitation, several hands went up—I turned to the board, figured out the name of one of the hands, Jane, and asked her to make me a seating chart. Then I told them that I would be teaching them English, Math and Science. This announcement was followed by groans…I was losing them, so I launched into telling them about my very recent experiences in the US Army. I allowed that I thought most teachers were boring when I was in school. I asked how many classes had they suffered through in English—specifically grammar.

"Almost every day!" said Ronald. "We hate grammar," agreed the rest of the class by nodding and groaning.

"Well you won't hate it this time—grammar is going to be easy and fun," I boasted.

Actually I had no clue about how to teach grammar. I had been bored and disinterested during grammar classes as a student. I recall thinking, "come on brain, think of something, trust your brain…"

"OK, grammar tomorrow, and I promise we'll be done with it all in four weeks."

"For the whole year?" asked Ronald.

"Guaranteed." I was in trouble, but fortunately the bell rang and it was time for Science.

Although they did admit that they had Science, English and Math texts, only a few had them in school, and again I was forced to improvise. Hence I told them the story of my building a submarine which won a prize in the school science fair (when I was in the eleventh grade). I also told them in detail about my brother Dan and I blowing the submarine to smithereens. They were hooked. I sensed that as long as I could be interesting, there would be no discipline problem. It was a good beginning, but I was worried about keeping it going. These kids were pros at destroying teachers, and the pressure to keep them interested and under control was constant. I was beginning to realize that teaching young people is the toughest job there is. I had been in the classroom only one day, and I had a total of 97 student's names to learn and identify with faces, abilities, and problems, plus the Principal to satisfy, the parents to satisfy, and the faculty to work with or against, and the peripheral school board members and the maintenance personnel—all part of what seemed to be a huge unwieldy team.

And I had to come up with an exciting, original approach to teaching grammar—by tomorrow.

I had no lesson plan. Although I did know the basics of proper English grammar, I had never taught it. My guide was Warriner's Complete Guide to English Grammar and Composition: a repetitive and boring series of texts, still the best and most complete guide I know of…but it came to me as class was starting: most people are visual learners, and most people learn better, faster, when they are participating.

The next day in class the kids were actually sitting in their seats, waiting for me to do something, and I knew that they would not continue to sit and wait…I had about sixty seconds. I thought, what were they interested in…then the light went on.

"Ronald, please come up to the board and draw a car."

"What?" Ronald shook his head slowly.

"What, Mr. Wilkinson?" I would continue to work on this form of address for the rest of the year.

"What, Mr. Wilkinson— do you mean a real car?"

"Yes, Ronald, a car with all of its parts…can you do it, or should I ask someone else?"

Several hands went up. Ronald headed for the blackboard, picked up a piece of chalk, said "I can do it."

He quickly drew a boxy side-view of a basic car that was about twenty-four inches long.

"Good," I said, " but it needs to be much bigger. Please erase it and make it really big"

Ronald nodded, erased the first drawing and drew a car that took up almost all of the board.

"Great," I said.

Judy had her hand up, so I called on her. "Yes, Judy?"

"You know my name?"…I looked at her…"ah, Mr. Wilkinson."

"Yes, Judy. I know all of your names." (I had spent two hours last night memorizing the seating plan and names) "What is your question?"

"I thought this was English class…you know, grammar and stuff. This looks like drawing class…not even good drawing ".

I smiled and allowed the class to laugh. "You are right. Thanks for reminding me that we need to do grammar."

The class groaned.

"Does anybody know how many parts of speech there are?"

"Yeah, hundreds" came a mumbled answer from the middle of the room.

"Who said that?" I softly asked.

There was a moment of silence and Judy looked at Johnny which gave him away, so I asked: "Johnny, do you know one?"

Judy leaned over and whispered loudly, "Noun."

Johnny said, "Noun," and smiled hesitantly.

"Good," I said, "What is a noun?"

"That, that thing I drew on the board...the big car.." volunteered Ronald.

"Great," I said again, "Who has good handwriting?"

Mary raised her hand. "Mary, please write what Ronald just said on the board and print the word NOUN in big print over the drawing."

Mary did this

"Good, " I said. "Now we know one part of speech. A car or even a drawing of a car, is a noun.

"This is..." I frowned at Mary. She stopped in mid-sentence and asked, "What did he say?"

"That, that thing I drew on the board...the big car"

Mary went to the board and wrote the sentence clearly, and when she was finished I said, "That is almost a sentence, an answer to a question, and it has five parts of speech in it, and there are only nine parts of speech to learn. I think we can finish off most of the grammar stuff in about ten days."

"I don't get it," said Peter.

"Here's the deal," I said. "I am going to give each of you another name...you will be called a part of speech. You know, a noun, adjective, verb, adverb, article, preposition, pronoun, conjunction or interjection."

"I don't get this at all, " said Ronald .

"You will," I responded.

I walked around the room and assigned each kid (now students) one of the nine parts of speech.

There were thirty two students in class that day, which meant I had four nouns, four verbs, four adjectives, four articles, four prepositions, four adverbs, four pronouns, four conjunctions.(Interjections I added in the next class.)

I thought: Wow. Now what do I do?...One minute left in class. "For homework you only have to learn about your own part of speech—yes I know, I did not tell you what a part of speech really is...we'll find out tomorrow when we make you into sentences. Just remember what you are."

As they left class I overheard Ronald saying to Peter, "I'm a verb—that's much better than being a prostitution!"

"I'm a preposition, not a prostitution, you dweeb!"

"Dweeb? I don't remember what part a dweeb is?"

OK, I thought. I need to refine this by tomorrow—it's going to be a long night!

And it was. I should have assigned the making of signs indicating parts of speech. Instead I wound up labeling thirty-two four by six inch cards. The next day I handed out the cards and started by lining up the proper parts of speech under Ronald's sentence which was printed on the blackboard.

We actually had fun doing this. Then Judy said: "Mr. .Wilkinson, you make one up with all of the parts in it."

Yikes, I thought..., I will try...

"Bang! Judy stomped her feet because she was angry at Tom who had given her a small serving of runny ice cream."

"What kind of sentence it that?" complained Victoria, " I don't know where to go."

"What are you?" I asked.

"I'm a preposition."

"OK, prepositions are words that tell you "where" or "when" or "what" and they are usually small words."

"Like—at, and of?"

"Yes," I said.

Ronald was the interjection. "Bang," he said, "I go first."

"Good, Ronald, stand up on the left side of the classroom. Now who is next?"

"I am," said Judy, who happened to be a noun. I explained she was also a proper noun and would start with a capital letter.

"She is not proper, I saw her stick her tongue out at you when you weren't looking," smirked Jimmy.

I allowed the class a moment of laughter and assigned Victoria to be the verb, "stomped."

As the class progressed I made sure to include all of the students, and the sentences became more complex. By the third day, the students were inventing sentences and exchanging parts of speech, so I expanded into assigning them related parts of the sentences. After two weeks they not only knew the parts of speech but also could pick out subjects, direct and indirect objects, objects of prepositions and even knew it was correct to say "just between you and me" and "it is I" and "that is she" and why these seldom used constructions were actually correct. Some liked being nouns or pronouns so that they could be objects, and many of the boys liked being verbs or interjections, and I had to change them around to keep up the interest. Because the class was so fluid, lesson plans were almost useless, but after two weeks these eighth graders knew basic grammar!

Best of all we were having fun in class and the learning stuck!. Some of the sentences they concocted were long, complicated and funny. I was wrong about it only taking two weeks. The class actually wanted to "do grammar," and we did it at least once a week until the year ended. The rest of the week was devoted to writing and reading. We took turns reading aloud, which became a favorite activity.

And very importantly I learned never to raise my voice unless absolutely necessary to get attention, and then only as one word interjections, such as: STOP! Then I would walk to the offending, disrupting or needy student and whisper in his/her ear. What I would say depended upon the situation and student. The quiet, individualized concern or reprimand worked far better than the loud, public chastisement...always.

As for the writing I, once again, had to develop a creative approach, which five years later became my first book: published by Educator's Publishing Service in 1967 as Let Them Write, which was(is) actually a teacher's guide to teaching writing. I re-wrote the writing book in 1980 as: The Joy of Writing. Both books are now out of print...perhaps I will re-do them one more time.

And yes. ..I did meet with the Principal after school—several times—and together, we all did survive the year, and I learned a lot about kids, the school, parents, administrators and other teachers.

I will always be grateful for and never forget Ronald, who forced me to think, to relate and to teach.

THE TROUBLEMAKER

RS Wilkinson

Wrestling team 1969

I taught English and coached Wrestling at The Brooks School located in North Andover, Mass. from 1964 through the 1965-66 school years. Frank Ashburn, the Headmaster, was the only school administrator that I encountered during my 50 years in the classroom, who actually listened to suggestions aimed at improving the school. ALL other administrators mistook suggestions for criticisms—hence the rule: make a suggestion and run the risk of being fired. I did remember Mr. Kenny's warning: "Stick your little neck out—chop,

chop," but being young and full of nine lives or at least thinking so, I kept sticking my neck out and exposing it to the trusty, rusty old job guillotine.

I started at Brooks as the Varsity Wrestling coach in 1964. I was thirty years old. The previous coach, named Beaver (I never met him, nor did I know his first name) had done an excellent job of teaching, coaching and exciting the boys. I was repeatedly informed that our coaching approach was dissimilar. I was not a whistle-blower coach, and led the boys by doing the fifteen minute killer matt-drill, groaning through all of the exercises with them, starting every practice with pushups, sit-ups, running in place and various wrestling "Moves". I wrestled with each team member every day, spending more time with the less capable wrestlers than with the potential champions. This approach produced a balanced team. Each boy was given a "write-up" outlining his strengths and weaknesses. This was done after each match…the boys loved the individual acknowledgement, and responded to the praise/criticism with renewed energy and commitment. I also recorded a running commentary on each match, which I later played back for the team. The result was that Brooks, for the first time, won the Class B wrestling tournament in 1964. (Many people said it was Beaver's team, which was partially true that first year.) We came in fourth the next year, in 1965, and won the Class B Tournament again in 1966 by an even larger margin. That year we traveled to the "New England Tournament," placing fourth—not bad for a small school with forty-five students in the senior class . Mike Hajjar, our heavyweight wrestler, won by a "PIN" in All of his matches: a "PIN " is the ultimate "game over" hold. And he was awarded the "Best Wrestler in the Tournament" trophy. Especially impressive, considering the competition from much larger schools and from the state of Pennsylvania where the sport of Wrestling was a major emphasis. At both Brooks and B&N, where I next taught, Wrestling was considered a "minor" sport, especially when compared with Basketball and Hockey and Crew and Baseball and Football.

While employed at The Brooks School, I also taught English and wrote my first book in 1966. Published in 1967, the book was a teacher's manual entitled <u>LET THEM WRITE</u>. Now long out of print: published by Educator's Publishing Service in 1967, Cambridge, Mass. The book was used by many schools in New England. The book contained samples of student writing, and focused on interesting writing assignments which were read aloud to the class: the approach was designed to develop skills in writing reading, presenting and public speaking. It fostered enthusiasm for creative and expository writing. Yes, it actually worked! The students enjoyed writing—even, handwriting—which is becoming a lost art in the age of computers and texting. The "hand" part of handwriting conveyed much of the personality of the person doing the writing: did the student write slowly, quickly, carefully, carelessly, legibly or illegibly—this too is gone.

As was I…having been offered a job teaching English and coaching Wrestling at The Browne and Nichols School. I was well known in the New England school "circuit" for three things: I coached championship wrestling teams, had written a book, and had a beard. Yes, amazing but true, I was the only faculty member in the New England teaching "circuit" with a beard! Really. During my ten years teaching and coaching in New England, I never met another bearded faculty member. The beard at The Brooks School caused quite a "stir". Several of the older faculty members openly disapproved of my beard—especially the faculty wives, who seemed curiously attracted to and repelled by the beard. I recall meeting with Frank Ashburn to "Discuss" the beard. As Headmaster, Frank had a unique method of management. First he sat back in the chair at his desk. Raised his eyes as if to ask: "What do you have to say?" then still saying nothing, he would wait, slowly reach into his pocket for his pipe, then, leaning to his right, slowly reach into another pocket for a pouch of tobacco, insert the pipe into the tobacco and push a small amount into the pipe, then he would lean to the left and pull his tamper out of another pocket and carefully tamp the tobacco into the pipe, finally he would strike a match and puff several times slowly expelling three puffs of smoke, then he would place the pipe in its pipe holder on the desk, lean back and raise his eyes again and pause expectantly. He knew full well that nobody could outlast him at keeping his mouth shut, so we invariably launched into our presentation while Frank just listened. He had taught me the rare skill of listening—making no sound, no "yes, unh huh, unh oh, OK, or mmmmmmm" sounds. Just listening. Such a powerful skill—Frank did this with everybody, which gave overwhelming power to his words when he did speak. Lacking all of the nods and encouraging or discouraging sounds that most listeners provide, we had no idea what his actual response would be.

I once suggested a change in an athletic policy regarding the awarding of Letters of recognition to eighth grade students for participation in the required athletic program. A small felt, green, letter "B" was only awarded to the eighth graders that had played in all of the games. At that level I felt that all of the students who had participated in practice and attended every game should have some recognition for their effort. I made my case while Frank smoked, then he asked:" How many of the faculty support your idea?" I boldly said: "A majority, Sir"

"Could you put this in writing and obtain signatures of those who support this proposal?"

"Yes, Sir"

"By next week?"

"Yes, Sir"

I obtained the signatures...(I still have a copy of this document) and presented it to FDA, as we called him, it was then presented to the faculty and accepted at the next faculty meeting...seems such a small, almost insignificant, improvement, yet...

I was spoiled: never during my next fifty years in education would I meet a good administrator, most of them were agonizingly inept, some were unable to make decisions, some made prejudicial decisions, all but FDA lived on flattery. They had all excelled at the "brown nose" path to success and management and skipped 'Listening and Leading.'

I clearly recall the "beard" incidents as symptomatic of prejudicial leadership . As I have mentioned, there were no beards or even goatees at Brooks or any other school that I knew of. Realizing that anything new in physical appearance, especially in the 1960's if it involved the length of hair or a beard, would be a subject of controversy thanks to the Beatles, I spoke with FDA about my desire to grow a "neatly trimmed" beard. I was starting my second year at

Brooks when we met in his office. I could tell by his frown and the extra puffs he took on the pipe that he disapproved; I had expected this. As he prepared his pipe and puffed, I launched into my presentation—no reaction. I mentioned Abe Lincoln, Jesus Christ as bearded men of character, honor and note—no reaction. Finally I stopped talking and Frank looked at me and said: "I would prefer that you did not grow a beard, but if you wish to, that is your prerogative." Then he stopped and said no more except: "I am pleased with your handling of the Wrestling team and with your classroom performance –is there anything else you wish to talk about?"

I took a deep breath and said: "Thank you, No Sir"

And that was that. I grew the beard.

I felt that The Brooks School was the epitome of what an educational institution should be: a well-run school with high standards that was open to supportable new ideas which could be presented to and be considered by the Headmaster, without prejudice.

In my third year at Brooks I was offered the positions of English teacher and Varsity Wrestling coach at B&N, my alma mater, which I accepted starting in the fall of 1966. I reported to B&N sporting my beard, and was met at the door by the Headmaster, Ed Pratt. Ed actually stood in the doorway and blocked my entrance to the building and said: "Wilkie, lose the beard by tomorrow or lose the job—(Ed had called me "Wilkie" since my first days at B&N as a ninth grade student)…he was not kidding. Having no other source of income, no inheritance, and no savings—I shaved the infamous beard. I had started off on the wrong foot, wearing the black cloak, or perhaps I had only one foot left, but I did teach and coach at B&N for three years…dragging behind me the memory of the now famous SPECTATOR—Basketball –court- victory, and noticed with some satisfaction in September that the gymnasium was indeed open on Saturdays.

During my first year coaching Wrestling at B&N, 1967, we won the New England Interscholastic Class B Wrestling Tournament—the first time ever for B&N. Then we won again in 1968—two years in a row—three years for teams that I had coached if we count the last year at Brooks as one of "my" teams. That Winter I was elected Head of the New England Interscholastic Wrestling Association. I was truly enjoying teaching; my writing book was being used as a teacher's guide at B&N and in many New England schools, and I overheard talk that a I was favored as a possible choice for Headmaster (Ed Pratt's retirement was known to be eminent). The future looked good until two events transpired in the Fall of 1968. The first was a critical game of the football season: we were to face our arch rivals. As a JV coach of football, I was included in a conversation involving Jack Etter, the varsity football coach and director of athletics; Ed Pratt, the Headmaster; and The School Physician, whose name I do not recall. The conversation involved a discussion: the pros and cons of playing our star running back, David. David was indeed our key player, but he had injured his hip and was not able to run at full speed. There was a debate over whether or not to inject David's hip with Novocain which would allow him to run with no pain. The physician said that as long as David was not hit on his hip, he should be OK, but if he were hit he could seriously injure himself because there would be no feeling of pain…it was a gamble. My opinion was not asked on this matter, but I voted: "no Novocain." I was overruled, with frowns and a warning that this conversation was strictly "off the record." David played with a numbed hip, and he was not hurt; he threw the game winning pass. We all exhaled in relief. None of us smoked a pipe, but there was significant smoke and a chill in the air. I could feel the black cloak wrapped around my shoulders.

Football season ended, Thanksgiving approached and a disastrous idea—a major change in scheduling—a proposal for improvement eked into a diabolical position: first place in my brain. I knew that the school had a policy which required all students to participate in athletics every day after school—only medically excused students were exempted. The school had an excellent arts facility, including a dark room, enlarger, potter's wheel, water color and oil painting easels and supplies, a well- equipped music area and a dramatics program: all of which were unused during the afternoon hours while athletics were required. I intended to propose at the pre-Thanksgiving faculty meeting that we vote to allow all students to choose one term per year not to participate in athletics, and to pick another activity to satisfy their afternoon participation requirement. I had spoken with most of the faculty about this proposal and a majority agreed with me. This proposal was unique in the respect that I was a three-sport coach: varsity wrestling, JV football, and JV baseball—I was a "jock"—not an "artsy-craftsy-wimpo". Jack Etter came up to me before the faculty meeting and said: "If you make your proposal at the faculty meeting, it will be the end of football (Jack was the Director of Athletics and the football coach at B&N) and I will get you fired." I was incredulous, and did not believe either statement. As it turned out he was right about getting me fired but wrong about football.

I was not aware the he and Ed Pratt were old drinking buddies. I made the proposal, which came within two votes of passing, in spite of significant opposition to the idea from Ed and Jack, and the fact that the vote was a "Raised-hands" vote rather than by secret ballot...As others did, I noted those who voted for and against the proposal. I still remember being surprised at several faculty members who voted against the proposal out of fear of administrative disapproval. With good reason, it turned out, because four days later I was told by Ed Pratt that my contract, which was simply a hand-shake deal, would not be renewed—I was fired. Ed called me into his office and said that the reason for my termination was: "You care more about the students than you do about the system." He totally misunderstood that my proposal was intended to improve both the system and the educational opportunity for the student. (Ed retired at the end of that year, 1969, and the new Headmaster instituted exactly what I had proposed.) A member of the board of Trustees, took me to dinner at Joseph's that winter, and said: "You are similar to Jesus Christ—good ideas, but ahead of your time"...a little like the stick your neck out analogy.—I have never given B&N money, but I did make several lasting contributions to the school in at least three areas: athletics, academics and policies regarding after school activities and eventually even beards!

My status of disfavor was reinforced when I was ironically" locked out" of the gymnasium that winter. The Wrestling Association had instituted an early morning "weigh-in" on the day of wrestling matches. We were allowed to record the weights of wrestlers as early as 7:15 on the day of interscholastic matches. This allowed the team members to have breakfast without the fear of being overweight and disqualified. Many of the boys would try to weigh exactly at the allowable maximum weight for their "class". There were eleven weight classes: starting at 110 pounds and running up to Heavyweight or unlimited class. Each wrestler was required to weigh at or under his weight class before competing—this assured that the wrestlers were competing with boys of equal weight—the skill of the wrestler would determine who won rather than the size, as is also the case in boxing. All of the other schools participating in this sport were open by 7:15 or the coaches were provided with keys to the gymnasium to facilitate the early weigh-in of wrestling teams. B&N was not open until 7:45—not enough time to complete the weigh-in procedure before the 8:00 school opening. I asked Ed Pratt for a key to the gym: request denied. I asked to have someone else open the gym: request denied. The boys, who were aware of the situation, had discovered that one of the outside doors to the basketball court, which gave access to the rest of the gymnasium, was usually unlocked because it needed to be slammed for the lock to catch. The team would arrive early, push the door open, and I would follow them into the weigh-in room at 7:15 and I would then certify and record their weights. I stopped requesting a key—we did not need one. Ed grew suspicious when I became silent and the complaining by the boys stopped. He assigned Dave Rich, the Superintendent, the job of sleeping in the gymnasium to "catch" me sneaking in. I had known Dave since 1949, my freshman year as a student at B&N. He often drove us to and from games in the school's "woodie" Ford station wagon. In 1952, when I had been knocked unconscious while playing football—out so cold that Bill Eliott (the football coach) later said he thought I was dead—Dave drove me to the hospital, bouncing around in the back of the old wagon. In 1969, one Friday morning as the boys pushed open the gymnasium door, Dave was waiting, saying: "All right Wilkie, hand over the key." We had no key, and the boys showed Dave how they had obtained entry. He did not believe them, and they had him shut the door, and then they pushed it open. It took three times to convince him that it was his fault for not checking the door—the door was indeed not latching. We had one meet left in the season, and the boys (now truly locked out of the gymnasium) showed up with breakfast in their hands, stuffed down their food, eating as they ran to class, and some of them were recorded as "late" to class by as much as a minute. I had rediscovered that if you really want to unite a team: give the members a common feeling of being unjustly discriminated against. The whole situation was a classic example of mismanagement. The B&N Black Cloak still exists for me: I am not listed as a former teacher; I am not alone in this, a former Head of School is not listed—the 2003 and 2008 School Directories both incorrectly depict the school as being Headless from 1941 through 1948) but I do get requests for donations.

Finally, and I do hope finally, the senior class in 1969, wanted to dedicate the Yearbook, "The Torch" to me.

The administration would not allow this, and the Yearbook was dedicated to Ed Pratt. However, the senior class bought a page in the yearbook, and although they were not allowed to include my name, the last page has a picture of me, with my infamous beard, and with comments contributed by the seniors. As it should be, the best memories and the best and longest lasting rewards stay with me from the students.

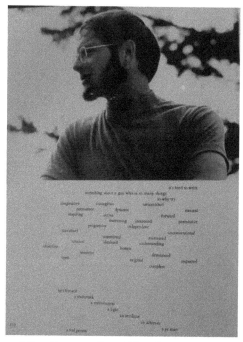

The Seniors Last Words on RSW

MOTHER'S GRAIN STORE 270

RS Wilkinson

Wilkinson's Feed Store was a combination grain and feed and hard-ware store. We all manned the store: Claire, Heather, Russel and Grace during the 1970's. Because we were farming and our need for everything that was farm related had blossomed out of control, we needed the store to supply ourselves. We had well over two hundred animals to feed if you counted 4 cows, one bull, four horses, two breeding pigs (sows and their piglets), sixty chickens, twenty ducks, several geese, three turkeys, two to six Alaskan Malamutes and two to four Doberman Pinschers, two goats and one very smelly Billy goat. All of the animals, oh yes I nearly forgot the rabbits, were breeders. To help pay the bills, Claire cleaned houses during the day and I taught high school English. The Feed Store was open from 11 to 6. The day started at 5 AM with chores: feed and water and check the animals, start cleaning the barn, get ready for school…then get to school: out the dirt road one mile to the school bus for the children (often walking during the winter). Claire stayed behind to milk and finish cleaning out the stalls. Then she drove Voltaire, our 1940 Chevrolet truck, out to her house -cleaning job. She used to say the barn was cleaner than the house—it was a clean barn!

I taught school in Farmington, NH, a drive of thirty miles each way, and Claire opened the store after her house-cleaning job(s). We were all in the store until 6PM, and then drove Voltaire, back the two miles to our house. I drove a 1960 Ford Falcon back and forth to school. I paid Clint Reed $10...that's right, ten dollars, for the nearly worn-out Falcon...I think he was going to junk the car if I didn't buy it. He thought ten dollars was more than fair—I drove the car for three years. After we closed the store we made dinner (mostly Clare did this but the kids were good about helping with everything from the cooking to doing dishes). Then we had farm chores again, finishing at about eight PM. Claire was by far the best at milking the cows.

You don't just squeeze the teats and get milk. First you sterilize the bucket, then you clean the cow's udder and teats with antiseptic solution. Then you tie back the cow's tail so you don't get whapped in the face. Balancing on the three-legged stool you tap the udder gently with the back of your hand (this emulates the nudges that a calf gives the mother prior to feeding) and talk to the cow so she knows who's there. Finally you squeeze the teat starting by closing your fingers progressively from the thumb and index finger down to the little finger. If the cow lets her milk down, you will get a stream of milk with each squeeze. If she doesn't like you, you get almost nothing. Figure on squeezing at least a thousand times to milk a cow dry. Our cows: milking shorthorns, a jersey and a Heinz 57 mix, would vary from two gallons to a half-gallon each milking—morning and evening. We drank a lot of the sweet, fresh, raw milk, and we agreed that bottled milk didn't even taste like milk. We also made cheese and yoghurt and sold some at the grain store. The cows HAD to be milked every morning and evening.

"Why?" asked Edgar, who was visiting one weekend.

"Because they make milk all of the time, and their udder gets full and hurts—just like when you have to go Pee," explained Russel.

"And if you're late at milking time, the cows MOO LOUDLY and they get restless and sometimes step in the milking pail—which is not good," said Heather.

"And then they swish their tails and hit you in the face when you try to milk them!" added Grace.

""Yuck. That's why I tie their tails to the stanchion," agreed Heather.

"That's why I would rather take care of the pigs," said Russel.

Claire said, "Tomorrow is Sunday, and Grammy is stopping at the store after Church and she wants us to stop by for dinner, so we'll try to close at 4PM, and wear your good clothes." Which meant clean.

Grammy was my Mother, seventy-five, and as mentioned in other chapters, was a frighteningly bad driver. She was driving a 1964 Oldsmobile 88 which had an automatic transmission and a big V8 engine. The car was "hot" which meant fast, not stolen.

Mother visited with us in the store, during which time she reminisced about her childhood…about the horse and buggy days. Mother was born in 1897. As it was Sunday, Mother chose to tell the story about her cousin, Madeline, and church. It seems that Madeline was taken to a church by Mother's mother. She had never been to this church before. It was an Episcopal Church, and after the service Grammy Jones, Mother's mother, asked the seven year-old Madeline what she thought of the priest? Madeline answered the question by saying: "He didn't pay no attention to me, so I didn't pay no attention to him!" For some reason, Mother thought this was very funny, and so did we. Mother did not like Madeline and often told us that the reason the priest didn't pay any attention to Madeline was that Mother was his favorite. Additionally we were never allowed to use incorrect English, and her quoting Madeline was the only time I remember hearing Mother speak incorrectly—and children simply did not talk back or answer questions in this impertinent way, certainly not to adults—which made it doubly funny to us. So much so that we all adopted Madeline's snippy response and used it whenever possible. Mother did have a good sense of humor, and occasionally even she would surprise us with a snippy comment, and on this particular Sunday she had not liked the sermon and answered my question : "how was the sermon today?" with the now famous response: "He didn't pay no attention to me, so I didn't pay no attention to him!"

Mother laughed and said she would return to her place on Province Mountain—which was seven miles from the store—to prepare dinner. The Feed Store was on the corner of a four way intersection. The car was parallel parked in front of the store and Mother needed to make a U-turn and then immediately a left turn at the intersection. A group of teenagers was standing across the street from us.

"It would be really nice if Russel could come with me to help with buying the chicken and starting dinner," Mother smiled sweetly. Russel was eleven years old and skillfully drove our tractor and truck on the farm. He liked driving, but looked sadly resigned about riding with Mother.

"You might want to fasten your seatbelt, Russ," whispered Grace.

I mentioned this because there was not yet a seatbelt law, and we only had a single lap belt in those days which we seldom fastened. Claire and I nodded in agreement, and Russel gave us the 'train is coming and we're parked on the tracks look'. Then he slowly turned and got into the passenger side of the front seat. I gave Russ my most encouraging smile and suppressed the sinking feeling of impending disaster.

Mother slipped into the driver's seat. She was five feet tall and could barely see over the dashboard—the picture of a sweet, white-haired old lady—turned the key and started the car in her normal manner, which was to depress the accelerator and race the engine while we prayed the motor would not fly into pieces. Then with her left foot stomping on the brake, she put the car into drive and floored the accelerator—her usual starting technique. The motor moaned and fought against the brakes, but the brakes won, and the car hunched down, quivering with all of its drive systems straining. Mother turned the wheels hard over to the left, looked out with a smile and lifted her foot off of the brake. SCREEEEECH! The rear wheels peeled, smoking, burning rubber, kicking up a huge cloud of dust and sand which nearly obscured the rear end of the car. The car lurched forward several feet but then almost instantly, screeched to a halt. I could see Russel spread up against the dashboard. Then Mother removed her foot from the brake, and the Olds lurched forward, spinning around in the middle of the road. Practically blinded by the dust, I watched as Mother smiled sweetly, waving out of her side window. The steering wheel, which she had released, spun wildly to the right and then again to the left and then and hard to the right, (as cars did before the dampening effect of power steering) . Mother was letting the car steer itself, which she often did. Russel's face was now plastered wide-eyed against the passenger window—he was either amazingly controlled or frozen in fear. Mother cranked the wheels hard left again and the Olds ground to a grinding stop for a moment, nose diving Russel up against the dashboard. Then, with smoking tires and gravel and sand flying she accelerated and zoomed through the intersection, heading perfectly, even in the correct lane, in the direction of her home.

"Holy shit!" yelled one of the kids standing on the corner as he waved away the cloud of dust and smoke. "That was fuckin' sensational. Where the HELL did that old lady learn to drive?"

"That was my Grandmother," said Heather, "years of practice— she always drives like that."

The boys stared after the disappearing car in admiration: "Wow! Can we ride with her sometime?"

"You can take my place anytime," said Grace. "You ought to ride with her to Church some Sunday—you'll learn how to pray— big time."

"Yes," nodded Heather, "She stopped a train in Burlyville one Sunday…coming back from church. Drove off the road coming down the hill to the RR tracks—Rt. 153 is a very "wavy" road with a sharp turn that runs down a small, steep hill to a Railroad Crossing. Grammy made it around the curve but could not possibly stop for the flashing red lights at the RR crossing…so she swerved off the road to the left, and went through somebody's front yard. She was trying to avoid those "annoying blinking red lights", and she was going way too fast to stop. We don't know how she missed three maple trees while doing a slalom course around them. Said she just released the wheel, closed her eyes and the car steered itself. It finally flew off a four-foot embankment and landed with a loud crunching noise followed by four gunshot-like explosions as all four tires blew out…right across the tracks in front of the train and next to the old train station, which she also narrowly missed. The station had been converted into a beauty parlor—you know, really a hairdresser salon. Well the ladies inside the parlor could not miss hearing the wail of the train whistle and the screeching of the train's brakes and the tires exploding, and they all ran out in various stages of drying and dripping hair expecting to see some wild-eyed drunken or drug-crazed teen ager, but instead, there sat Grammy clutching the wheel, white-haired, five foot tall, wearing her pretty, Daisy-decorated Sunday-go-to-church hat, which had become tilted crazily to the left during the episode, and attired in her favorite Spring, flowered dress. Grammy was smiling sweetly, at the engineer, who had miraculously stopped the train about one foot from the car. Later Grammy said he just stood there with his mouth hanging open—didn't say a word. You really sure you want to ride with her?" Heather looked up and smiled sweetly—just like Grammy!

The boys were also speechless—stuck their hands into their pockets, hunched up their shoulders and stood looking down the road—Grammy was long gone.

We didn't hear any sirens or crashing noises, so we all assumed that Mother and Russ made it to her place in one piece.

"Let's close a little early," I said. "Grammy likes ice cream. We'll stop and get desert."

" Better get three flavors though," said Grace. "You know if it is not her idea, she will turn down the first two!"

AND FINALLY, GIRLS AGAIN...

RS Wilkinson

And finally Sally did keep her promise of a favor that day. As she ran away from me her feet paddled awkwardly out side-to-side, and her blue, flower-print dress bounced up and down, and her hair swung left and right with the quick, determined jerky movement of youth, and then abruptly, she stopped…braking with first her right foot then her left, pausing a moment with both feet apart, and suddenly jumped up and spun around to face me—landing on both feet at the same time. She leaned toward me, hands upon her knees, smiled the almost straight-line, tight lipped, mischievous, crinkled eyed, flicker…drew her right hand slowly up to her face, pursed her lips and kissed its palm. Then she slowly turned her palm towards me, rotated it completely around, and bending her hand back level with the ground, palm up, softly blew the kiss.

DOES IT EXIST?

RS Wilkinson

In 1944 this conversation occurred among Peg, my sister, Dave and Dan, my brothers and me...Bob.

We were on the Province Lake beach. The month was August.

Peggy is 16
Danny is 6
Dave is 13
Bobby is 9

We are standing in a circle, about four feet apart on the lakefront beach, close to the water's edge.

Peggy: *Scooping up some sand and letting it fall gently through her fingers.* It does not!
Dave: Does too, but not really.
Dave: A lot depends on who gives it.
Bobby: It might as well be real; everybody knows about it if you have it.

But you can't see it, *insisted Peggy.* It disappears just like this sand.

Dave: You know if you have it.
Danny: Well, I never get it.

Peggy: Neither do I!

Dave: Yup…goody two- shoes—you're a girl. Daddy's favorite.

Bobby: So it does exist, otherwise you could not know you don't have it.

Peggy: Smarty pants! If you're so smart, how come you practically own it?

Bobby: See…gotcha. Another admission that it exists!

Danny: I don't get it.

Dave: That's right, you never get it.

Danny: What are you talking about?

Peggy: The Black Cloak…you wouldn't understand.

Danny: Yes, I would too!

Dave: No you wouldn't—I have it most of the time.

Bobby: No you don't. I have it more than you…right Peggy?

Dave: Don't ask her or Dan. They never get it, so they don't even know what it is.

Bobby: Oh yes they do—they cause it all of the time.

Dave: Not all of the time. Sometimes we deserve it.

Bobby: Not me! Don't look at me like that…OK, not I…Do we always have to use correct English?

Peggy: Yes, or you get the Cloak from Mother.

Bobby: There, see? You just admitted it exists again.

Dave: Sometimes you are a Royal Pain, Bobby. We all know it exists.

Bobby: Well then, get Peggy to admit it.

Dave: She's a girl. They never admit they're wrong—just like Mother.

Peggy: Not true!!

Dan, Dave and Bob all nod in agreement: Yes it is..really true!

Dave, turning around in frustration: You just have to let it go. Never argue with girls…

Bobby: Well…what if they're wrong?

Dave: Never mind—it's a waste of time. Probably get you awarded the Black Cloak.

Peggy: Keep talking like that and you'll really deserve the Cloak, and you can keep it forever.

Bobby: Jeeze! I win the argument and still lose!

Dave: Remember this…very important…typical loss to a girl.

Peggy in Dave's face: Sometimes I wonder why girls like you at all!

Dave: Simple. I'm not like Bobby…I care about the girl, not the argument.

Bobby turns slowly around in a circle to face Dave: I know, I keep getting stuck on the truth—I should keep my big mouth shut.

They all move over next to a canoe that is resting, upside-down on the beach.

Dave bends over to pick up a flat pebble, flings it out over the water where it skips and hops three times and sinks:

Then Dave says: Try doing it just like that pebble.

Bobby: Now I don't get it.

Peggy: I think I get it. Three tries and you're a goner—just like the pebble, *long pause*. It is like baseball…three strikes and you're out.

Dave: Close, but not really. Look, if you lean a little to the right, hold the rock flat side down, crooked into your index finger and throw it sidearm like this, you get more skips.

Dave leans and throws…, the rock skips four times and sinks.

Dave: See, sometimes you can even get five skips, but it is a rock. It will always end up sinking.

Dan: Duh, everybody knows this. Even I can get four skips.

Dave: Right, but trying to get more…to beat everybody else before you quit…it is the fun of winning.

Bobby: Even though everybody loses in the end?

Peggy: I get it.

Dave: What?

Peggy: We all die in the end…what counts is how many skips we do.

Dave: Yes. This is one reason why girls like me.

Danny: What does that mean?

Bobby: You're too young to know…I think. Go ask Mother.

Peggy and Dave together: No, no, no! We'll all get in trouble.
    Don't ever ask her anything like that!

Dave; Right, the Cloak is not big enough for all of us.

Bobby: Wanna bet?

Peggy: Stop it. Just let it drop.

Bobby: *Sarcastically:* You mean like the fourth skip 'cause you
    can't get it to the fifth one?

Danny: I can so…I just need a better pebble!

Bobby: Sorry, I wasn't talking to you, Dan.

Danny: No fair, you guys always leave me out!

Bobby: Now you know what it feels like…but you 'll never
    really know what it's like to have a younger brother.

Peggy: I said stop it! Let's walk to the Log Cabin and get some
    ice cream…if they have any.

The Log Cabin was truly a little log cabin with a small ice cream, hot dogs and chips store on one end.

And so we all turned and walked the one-half mile to the Log Cabin, and by the time we got there, we were talking about the Boston Red Sox and their impending, frustrating, annual demise at the hands of the New York Yankees. And all was well with the world of kids except for the fact that we were at war with Germany, and gasoline was rationed as were many food staples, including butter. Ice cream was not usually available unless it was homemade. Mrs. Hobbs had cows, fresh unpasteurized milk, and a centrifugal-force cream separator that she demonstrated for us. Thanks to her we often had fresh milk and could make real ice cream in our old hand-cranked White Mountain freezer. A tradition we kept for many years in the summers when we were in Maine.

We led dual lives, and during the school year lived in the Boston area where we had weekly air-raid drills involving school evacuations. The windows in our houses had blackout curtains (no lights showing at night) and the top half of car headlights were painted black so that there would be less light at night to identify cities, because bombing was done by visual identification. And every able bodied (which meant breathing in and out) adult was required to serve in the military. We were acutely aware of how precious and brief our childhood freedom would be. Fortunately for the whole world, the war ended in May of 1945: Victory in Europe Day, and Victory in Japan Day was July, 1945. We were again "at peace" and there was gasoline and even ice cream. This was the simple, orderly and peaceful world that so many men and women had fought to preserve.

But the best times were had during the summers at Province Lake…a lake which was split by the Maine/New Hampshire state line and bordered by a white, mile long, sandy beach on the south side. And before they tarred the road along the water's edge, the beach was clean and separated from the road by a slim line of trees and bushes…a haven for the few kids and adults who gathered there to swim and watch the spectacular sunsets. Now the beach is dirty, separated from the road by a 3 foot tall steel rail, but the view to the mountains in the North is still beautiful and unchanged.

And because the Log Cabin had no ice cream, we settled for a hot dog.

And now we jump forward: it is seventy one years later in 2015, and Dan and I walk the same beach again. Dave had been killed in an automobile accident on Hawaii in 1982 and Peggy succumbed to Parkinson 's disease in 2007, and Sam, my oldest brother, had died in 2010.

We are standing approximately where Dave was caught by Dad under the canoe in 1949.

Dan and I each pick up a small flat stone and look out over the water.

> Bob: How's your right arm, Dan? Think you can get three skips?
> Dan: Maybe. I'll give it a try. How's your left arm?
> Bob: Well, my left shoulder is shot…too much wrestling, football and high school pitching, but let's each try. Could tell us how many starts we have left .

Bob leans to the left and throws the pebble awkwardly…it skips twice.

Dan leans to the right and also throws, almost stumbles…it skips three times.

Bob: Good one Dan, but I think the Cloak hindered my throw!

Dan smiles.

Dan: Well I have to admit, it probably did.
Bob: There is one thing though…would you mind?
Dan: Not at all…you mean the Black Cloak?
Bob: Yes.

Bob turns his back to Dan, who slowly unfastens the invisible cloak, carefully pretends to fold it, and gently places it on the beach

MY BROTHER, DAN, THE KEEPER

RS Wilkinson

Another good memory

My brother, Dan, looked up at me with the trusting, open eyes of a six year old and asked: "Is this a keeper?"

"Yes," I answered, with the absolute certainty of a nine year old..."But, you will have to chop off the head, remove the guts and scrape off the scales and remove all of the little bones to..."

Splash! The 10" perch flashed away to freedom.

"Guess not" said Dan. And that was that. Another part of the long-lost, simple world of childhood that we now hold dearly as memories…the "Keepers."

Together, we owned a 1929 Model A Ford, which we restored (although it did not need much)—I bought Dan out and took the car to Middlebury College in 1954…no defroster and no heater meant cold, cold in the Winter. I had to let it go.

Dan spotted a 1917 Model T Ford in a barn in Sanbornville, NH. We fixed it up (it only needed tires, a new top –and some uphol-stery work because it had 2,400 miles on it!) We sold the Model T to a doctor we met by chance at a Richards Drive-in Carfeteria. The doctor was driving a new Porsche, but we were surrounded by girls wanting a ride…wonder if he kept the car…wonder if the girls were attracted to us or the car??? Better not to know…

Dan, you are the keeper of the family: you have kept, cate-gorized, organized and shared the family memories stored on film, slides, photographs and sound tapes…hours, literally days, even weeks, devoted to preserving and sharing the past and the ever changing present.

You are the keeper of current relationships, and just as with the Model T, the fixer of worn-out relationships, and lost or cast aside parts.

Dad taught us how to hand crank the Model T: sometimes it would backfire, especially if the "timing" was retarded. If you were not holding the crank correctly, it would spin backwards and break your wrist. Even if you held the crank correctly, a backfire would hurt, but the main thing was that you were still able to crank it again until the engine started.

Well, there have been a number of "backfires" in this family, Dan, many of which I may have caused, and many of the tires are worn out or just plain flat, and some of us may never be in balance, or never have been, and our timing may be off, but there is one sure thing: you are the best Brother and you are the " Keeper."

Love you, Dan, Bob.

ABOUT THE AUTHOR

Still standing at eighty

Bob Wilkinson's eighty years covers a lot of ground and water. He was born and grew up in the Boston area, earned A.B. and M.A. degrees from Middlebury College in Vermont and served in the U.S. Army as a guided missile repair and calibration specialist. He taught English and Writing for 45 years at the secondary and college levels and wrote *LET THEM WRITE,* a teacher's manual, published in 1967 by Educators' Publishing Service, Inc. He and Claire, his wife, designed and built a house and barn employing only hand tools, and farmed in Maine for twenty years...living without electricity. Then they designed and built, in Florida, from scratch, CLAIRE MARIE, a 35-foot sailboat. After sailing and racing her for ten years, they embarked on a disastrous trip to the Bahamas and the Virgin Islands. Bob now lives in Bridgton, Maine where he is restoring an old house and barn and writing stories and playing the Blues.

In addition to *THE BLACK CLOAK*, Bob is nearly finished with another book, *THE DEVIL IN THIN WATER*: the unique story of how a gross of "rubbers" kept him and his motley crew supplied with food, ice and ice cream while shipwrecked in the Bahamas.

Bob may be reached at: smokingwoodstove@gmail.com

Printed in the USA
CPSIA information can be obtained
at www.ICGtesting.com
LVHW080801090124
768362LV00027B/1620